JANE AUSTEN'S NOVELS

Social Change and Literary Form

Julia Prewitt Brown

HARVARD UNIVERSITY PRESS
Cambridge, Massachusetts, and London, England 1979

Publication of this book has been aided by a grant from the
Andrew W. Mellon Foundation

Library of Congress Cataloging in Publication Data

Brown, Julia Prewitt, 1948-
　　Jane Austen's novels.

　　　Bibliography: p.
　　　Includes index.
　　　1. Austen, Jane, 1775-1817—Criticism and inter-
pretation.　I.　Title.
PR4037.B73　　　823'.7　　　78-16879
ISBN 0-674-47172-5

TO DEAVER

Acknowledgments

I should like to thank Michael Wood and Carl Woodring for reading an earlier version of the manuscript and for their ideas, criticism, and encouragement. I am also grateful to the late Lionel Trilling, Brian Southam, Patricia Craddock, Helen Vendler, Catharine Stimpson, Ellen Moers, Richard Goodman, Laura Wexler, Garrett Stewart, Virginia Prewitt, and Michael McKeon for reading the manuscript and for giving me their suggestions and support. To my friend Carol McGuirk I am especially thankful for ideas and conversation about Jane Austen, and for her generous response to every draft. Finally, I should like to thank Deaver Brown, who helped me at every stage of the writing of this book, for his criticism, enthusiasm, and support.

Contents

This is an important book the critic assumes,
because it deals with war. This is an insignificant
book because it deals with the feelings of women
in a drawing-room.

Virginia Woolf

An Introduction
to the Novels

To many readers, the idea of social change would seem inconsistent with Jane Austen's concerns. It is commonly held that she was ignorant of the "great world," of history and poverty and royalty, and that her ignorance dictated her choice of a domestic subject. This is like saying that Leonardo da Vinci painted the *Mona Lisa* from a merchant's wife because he could not get a duchess to sit for him. And it presupposes an antithesis between women and history, between domesticity and history, and between the self and society that Jane Austen's novels do not confirm. As the first great woman author in England, Jane Austen gave meaning to domesticity for the first time in English fiction. Her novels are the first to fully assert the cultural significance of marriage and family, their role in social and moral change.

In general, Jane Austen's criticism has been unreceptive to the great significance with which she invested her subject.[1] This attitude comes from the limitations of traditional historiography and aesthetics. Our histories are only beginning to comprehend the role of domesticity; our aesthetics is derived from the Aristotelian hierarchy of subject matter and theory of catharsis, with which the English novel in general and Jane Austen's novels in particular are incompatible. These historical and aesthetic biases merge in the commonplace view that Jane Austen is not a great novelist because her subject matter is too "restricted"—that is, historically insignificant or emotionally shallow.

These biases help to explain the misconception of Jane Austen as an unconscious artist, as one whose genius was merely employed in recording the life around her, which happened to be that of the English gentry at the end of the eighteenth century. This view was quite prevalent in the nineteenth century, even in the criticism of

Henry James, and is all the more surprising when one considers how conscious an artist Austen clearly is. Unless we view the broad, self-deprecating irony of her earliest works as an aberration, we must assume that Jane Austen was highly attuned to the unheroic implications of her subject from the beginning of her career. In the opening sentences of *Northanger Abbey* she delights in the eccentricity of this choice and anticipates the condescension of her audience: "No one who had ever seen Catherine Morland in her infancy would have supposed her born to be an heroine. Her situation in life, the character of her father and mother, her own person and disposition, were all equally against her." The sentimental novel is not the sole target here; Austen is challenging the Western tradition of heroism itself. The ancient hero is known to be a hero at birth; and, according to Aristotle, heroes and heroines must be nobler in appearance and mind than average, and even taller than most mortals. Catherine Morland, however, has "by nature nothing heroic about her." Her parentage, appearance, and intellect are all confirmedly average. We learn on the first page of the novel that her father "had never been handsome" and her mother "had a good constitution." Her destiny is merely marriage.

Emerson, exasperated by such deliberately uninspired material, issued just the complaint Austen had anticipated: "Suicide would be more respectable." It is precisely this question that *Northanger Abbey* poses. Austen knew that to modern, romantic taste, or to the first generation of readers of *The Sorrows of Werther,* suicide *is* more respectable than conventional marriage. Gothic literature had vulgarized this sensibility, but Austen wanted her readers to see themselves in Catherine Morland. "Are they all horrid?" she asks, wishing to be assured of the gothic novels she is about to read. "Are you sure they are all horrid?" Catherine's thirst for horror is really no different, Austen implies, from her own reader's boredom with Mrs. Morland's "good constitution." "[Instead] of dying in bringing [Catherine] into the world," she apologizes, "Catherine's mother lived on to have six more children."

Austen's irony does not of course completely answer Emerson's complaint, or the complaint of any reader who finds her subject matter shallow. Much modern criticism of Jane Austen has tried to make it answer, and is consequently more ingenious but less appreciative of her actual subject matter than nineteenth-century criticism was. In the words of Ian Watt, the attitude peculiar to this century is that "Jane Austen is first and foremost a critical observer of humanity who uses irony as a means of moral and social judgment, who enlarges the reader's understanding of experience through making him realize how limited is that of her fictional characters."[2] Not surprisingly, the final judgment of Watt's excellent essay recognizes that to be conscious that something is trivial does not justify its triviality.

Freud has said, and I think rightly, that we seek in the world of literature compensation for the poverty of life. There we find people who know how to die, or to experience that which we are terrified to imagine. There we discover the plurality of lives for which we crave, for we die in the person of a given hero and yet survive him.[3] The mastering of anxiety that Freud identifies as the function of literature is not unlike the cathartic satisfaction formulated by Aristotle. What compensation, then, can we find in the novels of Jane Austen? Her world is a customary world, a world in many ways alien to the one poets and dramatists have traditionally shown us. Even the sentimental and picaresque fiction that preceded Jane Austen was heroic, for although its characters were not universalized, its subjects often were; and novels like *Robinson Crusoe* and *Clarissa* gave readers the emotional satisfaction of seeing ordinary people like themselves experience an absolute.[4] In the world of Austen's fiction, however, birth, death, passion, and God are only reported realities; is nothing experienced that could allow us to temporarily transcend the consciousness of our destiny?

Many readers have found her novels intractable to such demands. An English writer, questioning the spiritual depth of the English novel in general, cried out half-humorously: "Who cares whether Pamela finally exasperates Mr. B. into marriage? whether Mr. Elton is more or less than moderately genteel . . . whether the District Officer's fiancée ought to see so much of Dr. Aziz . . . ? Who cares?[5] Novels of course tell us much more about life than the exasperated critic implies, as Lionel Trilling has shown in his eloquent essay, "Manners, Morals, and the Novel." The novel, he explains, is "a perpetual quest for reality, the field of research being always the social world, the material of its analysis being always manners as the indication of the direction of man's soul."[6] Yes — but is this a full explanation of Jane Austen's method and achievement? No matter how complicated appearances are, no matter how complex the interweaving of manner and soul in a given character, and no matter how luminous the web of reality manifested, we may still feel that the action of that soul is somehow deficient: deficient to the claims of art, and deficient to the demands of the human imagination. According to E. M. Forster, "All the Jane Austen characters are ready for an extended life, for a life which the scheme of her books seldom requires them to lead."[7] In the eighteenth century, the characters of Richardson, Fielding, and Sterne lived out their extended lives in wider spheres of feeling, adventure, and imagination. In the next century, in the works of Dickens, Thackeray, and Eliot, the individual was often seen as a "case" representing a larger sociohistorical situation. And while in her later novels Jane Austen does make large connections with the events and conditions of the time, she carefully underplays them, and her last novel remains outwardly as unambitious as the first. However tightly bound by circumstances, no individual in Jane Austen ever becomes a "case."

Forster's statement may be used to formulate some central questions concerning Jane Austen's subject. Are the lives of her characters really lived, or do they remain untested, unrealized? Is marriage to Darcy an adequate destiny for Elizabeth Bennet? Do Emma's offenses at Box Hill deserve such high status as moral actions in the story? Or for that matter, are the lives led by all the heroines proportionate to the complex presentation of their personalities and situations? Is this world of parties, picnics, and country dances at all meaningful in itself?

The following pages will show why the answer to these questions is yes. The picture of ordinary, middle-class domestic life that nineteenth-century readers found so convincing is not merely a convenient background for a comedy of manners and values, meant to teach us the limitations of our own lives. It constitutes, rather, a foreground of social and moral change, conceived with an irony that accurately reflects its tensions.

Austen's novels expose the transition into the nineteenth century. The eighteenth-century novel, derived from allegory and romance, still sought to define social experience in relation to an absolute. Robinson Crusoe's retrospective belief in the hand of Providence, Clarissa's culminating death, and Tom Jones's unrepentant good fortune all provide a metaphysical frame for the action in their novels, however many social questions are raised against that frame. The frame disappears in Jane Austen, and its absence explains why proportion is a central question of her art and the basis of her irony, and why transcendence is unavailable to her reader. (The opening of *Northanger Abbey* shows that Austen aimed to deflect her reader's hunger for the compensations Freud describes.) At the same time, Austen only gradually adopted the nineteenth-century mode of making the individual the yardstick, the absolute, by which social experience is measured and judged. We see this beginning to happen in *Mansfield Park,* in which the world of the Mansfield estate and family is virtually brought into being with the arrival of the heroine, who becomes the moral yardstick for all that follows. In *Persuasion,* nineteenth-century individualism (or estrangement) is further established in the novel's form and content, as I will show. And *Persuasion* makes us see what later novelists could not have shown us as well — or what was lost in the emergence of individualism. We see the social and moral necessity for a democratic individualism that nonetheless meant powerlessness and alienation for the heroine, perhaps for women in general.

In her representation of this transition, Jane Austen alternated between two structures, comedy and satire. The form of the ironic comedies (*Northanger Abbey, Pride and Prejudice,* and *Emma*) has its source in the social situation of the eighteenth century and reveals the influences of Sterne and Fielding. The works of satiric realism (*Sense and Sensibility, Mansfield Park,* and *Persuasion*) look forward to a nineteenth-century social situation and anticipate the structure of novels by Thackeray, Dickens, Meredith, and Eliot. Jane Austen's vacillation between these two structures and her attempts to merge them do not reflect a mere involvement with form. On the contrary, they show that a fundamental shift in human relations was taking place during Jane Austen's lifetime.

Despite this structural contrast, Austen's novels are basically alike in their representation of social life. Each makes domestic life its center. Without faith in either Providence or individual will, Jane Austen chose concrete social relations as the place to make an argument. This argument has to do with the autonomy, the self-generating capacity of social relations in themselves—in particular, the power of marriage to bring together inner and outer experience, the self and the world. She was the first novelist to make such an argument, and as I will show, she was perhaps the last.

Marriage: The Subject

All of Jane Austen's novels end in marriage, "the origin of change."[8] Her subject is marriage, or how changes in the life of the society are brought about through selective mating. The parties, picnics, and country dances are the preparatory rites of marriage, and in their complex discriminations an ethic of selection is formed. The object of many of the taboos and restrictions that modern readers often deplore is the guarding of this chief act of life, marriage and sexual function, from interference.

To Jane Austen, this process of selection and marriage required no justification. Because the individual lived in the society and accepted it as the environment of his expression, his actions had social significance. Elizabeth Bennet's life could never be lost, like Dorothea Brooke's, in the plurality of "Theresas." To the extent that later writers often contemplated their characters as "cases," as John Bayley has said, the characters could be viewed, and often were, as "remarkable" or "unremarkable" cases.[9] There is a curious contempt for individual life in many nineteenth-century novels. Dorothea Brooke, Julian Sorel, Emma Bovary, and Isabel Archer are all seen as small and inconsequential compared to the huge social forces they encounter. In *Persuasion,* Jane Austen begins to share in this perspective. In her other novels, however, the individual person is always remarkable and requires no justification. *Emma* itself is about the irrelevance of justification. The heroine's actions are unjustifiable, but the heroine is not.

The gratuitousness of justification also comes from Jane Austen's belief that the marriage of ordinary persons is full of meaning and consequence. To Jane Austen, the selection of spouse is of crucial importance to the individual and society, for the individual is the agent of a social purpose, which is the moral education of children, and of younger persons in general—children who in their turn will rear and educate children. The wisdom of selection is imperative, for this one act contains the lessons of the past and the hopes of the future. The commonplace matter of Jane Austen's novels, then, has much to do with the possibilities inherent in ordinary existence; each story exhibits a kind of cultural and moral eugenics.

Jane Austen's conception of marriage is unique even though it reveals the influence of her predecessors. She draws on Richardson, for example, but alters his view of marriage and feminine life in crucial ways. In *Pamela* Richardson gives no indication that Pamela's spirit demands anything more than a marriage ceremony, the legalization of her sexual and social aspirations. At the close of the novel she is totally satisfied. Even in *Clarissa* and *Sir Charles Grandison* marriage is viewed as a final experience, the apotheosis of the spirit, and therefore as requiring an almost impossible purity of motive. In Jane Austen, the choice of a husband is bound up in all sorts of actual difficulties: in the heroine's decisions about herself and her future and her adult posture. The first encounters with her future husband mark the beginning of the heroine's moral growth, and her marriage is a stage in this growth. Pamela perhaps finds her way into Jane Austen's novels, but in adolescent characters like Lydia Bennet. The prototype of Austen's heroines may be found in the works of women novelists of the late eighteenth century, such as Fanny Burney, who, as Q. D. Leavis said, "provided her with a moralistic tradition—with crude models for those subtle discussions of matrimonial relations, filial obligations, right feeling and so on."[10] Yet

Fanny Burney's picture of social life is more or less restricted to social comedy and lacks the fabric of thought that underlies Austen's comedy.

All Jane Austen's novels involve three generations: past, present, and future. The past is exposed for its connection with the present, and in the decisions of the present the future is implied. *Pride and Prejudice* opens with a view of the parent generation and closes with a glimpse of the future married life of Elizabeth and Darcy, with Georgiana Darcy included as surrogate daughter. Among the novel's last words is a recognition of the effect of this new marriage on Georgiana: "Her mind received knowledge which had never fallen her way before"(*PP*, p. 388). The moral center of the novel lies in the connection between the parent generation and the present generation; the latter's actions are the subject of the novel's action. In the choice of spouse the men and women of the present either comprehend the lessons of the past or perpetuate its defects. Part of the problem is that the present generation unwittingly inherits the temperamental and moral deficiencies of its parents. Elizabeth possesses her father's ironic complacency; until she acknowledges this inheritance, she is unable to see clearly enough to make an adult choice of husband: "And yet I meant to be uncommonly clever in taking so decided a dislike to him, without any reason. It is such a spur to one's genius, such an opening for wit to have a dislike of that kind. One may be continually abusive without saying anything just; but one cannot be always laughing at a man without now and then stumbling on something witty" (*PP*, pp. 225-226). And through Elizabeth's influence, Darcy comes to face his own similarities to Lady Catherine: "I was given good principles, but left to follow them in pride and conceit" (*PP*, p. 369). The psychological tension of character in Jane Austen is frequently based on the battle between will and origin. Contrary to what D. W. Harding has said, there are no "spontaneous heroines" or villains in Jane Austen, no people whose moral character seems to have no origin.[11] Even Wickham has a spendthrift mother, and Mr. Collins a tyrannical father. The sources of personality, so constant a concern in *Mansfield Park,* are almost always understood by means of some complex interaction of factors; sex, status within the family, physical appearance, inherited temperament, and education all act on one another to produce a certain moral disposition. Jane Bennet's passivity results partially from her beauty, from the reassurance it has brought her. Mary Bennet's pedantry is the result of her plainness, and a defense against unpopularity. Who can doubt the source of Elizabeth's unabashedness, of Emma's self-indulgence? Even Anne Elliot turns out to be a true Elliot in the end by persuading herself she was right in taking Lady Russell's advice. We have only to recall Sir Walter Elliot's adeptness at persuading himself of his financial stability, and the disappearance of Mrs. Clay's freckles.

Family is the abiding reality of Austen's world: relations within families and, through marriage, relations between them. Family is the opening concern of every novel except *Northanger Abbey* (which Austen originally entitled *Catherine*) and *Emma,* the two novels that focus on the individual, as the titles suggest. The first chapter of *Pride and Prejudice* reveals the parents of the generation the book will examine. Not only are the parents the psychological and moral source of their daughters' personalities; they also set the example of adulthood and marriage for them, and ostensibly are to provide them with advice and aid. It has frequently been remarked that none of the heroines can look to her parents (or surrogate parent) for guidance. The importance of family in Austen's fiction has also been recognized but the connection between these two ideas has never been clarified. It is just this inadequate preparation and aid by the elders that makes the child's initiation into the adult world so difficult and dangerous. Elizabeth, Jane, and Lydia must depend entirely on themselves. At the same time each is unknowingly acting on the deficient values and attitudes derived from their parents. The achievement of "rational happiness" seems to depend on one's ability to separate oneself from a defective origin. Lydia's real failure is a lack of the fortitude necessary to forming one's own identity; instead she is resistlessly submerged by the power of mutual identification with her mother. In the choice of a husband, the choice with such far-reaching effects, her identity and her future are fixed.

Many of the fine studies of the structure of *Pride and Prejudice* affirm beyond all else the enormous significance of the moment of reconciliation, the final choice of spouse. Their analyses of the relationship between incidents, the illustration of how every dialogue, every event — indeed, even the language itself — leads up to the reconciliation and is indispensable to it, reveal how much is contained in this moment, how all time is compressed by this moment's ability to comprehend the past and imply the future. The continuity of life lies in the ritual of marriage. The hero and heroine need not bear children in the course of the novel; the cycle has already been set in motion through the novel's exposure of their relations to their own parents.

They need not, in fact, bear children at all, for in Austen's novels marriage confers a moral status upon the couple that gives them responsibility for younger persons in general. Georgiana Darcy can live with her brother at the close of the novel because he is married; Lydia can go to Brighton with Mrs. Forster because Mrs. Forster is recently married. The care of unmarried young people is an important issue at some point in each of the novels, and serious problems frequently result from deficient protection. The power to direct and guide younger members of society as well as one's own children makes responsible marriages a social and moral necessity. Perhaps more significant, surrogate parents are necessary in society because natural parents are dead (Lady Russell takes Lady Elliot's place) or, more frequently, deficient (Mrs. Gardiner takes Mrs. Bennet's place).

Jane Austen's belief that sex roles cannot be viewed from private perspectives is undoubtedly uncongenial to modern attitudes. It should be pointed out, however, that Austen does not view the limitation on individual freedom that a socially responsible marriage demands as unnatural or degrading. Dorothy Van Ghent would have us view the social life of *Pride and Prejudice* as a kind of Darwinian struggle for subsistence in the economic sphere.[12] This view holds some truth, but it would be more true if Van Ghent did not exclude the possibility of the individual's inward striving for a meaningful social existence.

Jane Austen sees individuals and classes as instinctively and problematically adaptable. The social philosophy that underlies all her work is founded on this belief in the cooperative end of human struggling. Selection of spouse is the central act for both sexes in the novels because it represents the vital opportunity for individuals to cooperate with one another and to adjust and improve their existence. Mr. Bennet's failure to regard the choice of mate as a serious decision costs him the "rational happiness" his daughter is wise enough to secure. The mating process is very closely connected to family: relations within families, such as the relationship between Elizabeth and her father, and relations between families, such as that between the Woodhouses and the Knightleys. The raising of the moral level of the "group," of society itself, is the end toward which the novel's action struggles. It is surprising how little depth Austen critics tend to attribute to these pivotal concerns. Despite the evident importance of adequate parenthood to both sexes, its preparatory operations, courtship and marriage, are traditionally regarded as feminine concerns, and by extension as historically insignificant. Such concerns do indeed make up a feminine tradition in our culture, a tradition of which Austen's novels are the first revolutionary expression. A clearer understanding of the conceptions of sexuality and marriage within this tradition may help to explain some of the more misleading preoccupations of Austen criticism.

Marriage has historically performed a complex function in feminine destiny: it establishes economic security and social status; through children, it provides a professionless class with an occupation that is potentially meaningful to the individual and a practical necessity to the society; it answers the psychic need of any vulnerable social group for a securely identified place in the universe, almost a refuge from it, where role and function are already provided; and until the present century, it has made the sexual experience acceptable to the majority of intelligent women. It is not surprising, then, that Jane Austen should view the selection of spouse as a complicated and crucial undertaking. The state of marriage was not only essential to a tolerable existence for most women (as Charlotte Lucas well knew); it was, for the English girl of Jane Austen's day, "the one time in her life when her destiny lay not in her family's hands, or in her husband's, but to a significant degree in her own."[13] Ironically, Jane Austen's novels show that the period of courtship was the least frivolous period of a woman's life, the one moment in which her entire future—social, emotional, and economic—was decided.

Two well-known preoccupations in popular and critical views of Jane Austen are explained by a failure to take into account the complexity of her notion of marriage. One is the concern that Jane Austen overvalued the "mercenary" motive in the choice of husband, a complaint that has appeared on and off from Walter Scott to Marvin Mudrick; another is the criticism of Austen's lack of treatment of sexual love. For a woman of Jane Austen's day, the choice of husband was analogous to the man's choice of profession; it involved practical and personal considerations, and the woman's view of her success in choosing was intimately bound up in her self-esteem. The full individual in Jane Austen has legitimate concerns other than passion and love in the choice of spouse *or* profession.

In a social tradition that dictates assumption by the woman of her husband's name and social status upon marriage it is inevitable that the man should take on the accoutrements of an institution in the woman's eyes and that the selection of a husband should therefore become a practical and moral enterprise. A frequent motif in literature by women may be understood in this light—the motif of male injury, of the damaging or reduction of the hero before he is capable of love. (Consider Mrs. Gaskell's *North and South,* Charlotte Bronte's *Jane Eyre,* and even, in the moral sphere, *Pride and Prejudice.*) This reduction signifies a kind of demystification of the male, a dissociating process that separates him in the eyes of the woman from institutions that seem changeless and impenetrable to her. In *Pride and Prejudice* the ethic of selection is established by a gradual stripping away of the institutional authority of the heroine's suitors (Collins and Darcy) to expose the moral substance or nullity beneath.

The other common criticism of Jane Austen is the exclusion of sexual love from the novels. (In the more dated studies, this is tastelessly explained by her spinsterhood.)[14] Although I think most readers would agree that the heroes and heroines are attracted to each other, that sexual suggestion is subtle and frequent, that Marianne's feeling for Willoughby reaches the level of a passion, and that the feeling between Anne Elliot and Captain Wentworth is a passionate tenderness, something in Austen's valuation of sexuality still denies it an exclusive eminence. To women before this century sexuality could have no exclusive significance. Before contraception became available to the majority of the middle class, the sexual experience was intimately connected with conception in the minds of literate women. (Tolstoy reveals his awareness of the impact of contraception on the feminine self-concept by his mention of it in *Anna Karenina*.) Since no social provision was made for women who bore children outside of marriage, let alone for illegitimate children, it is understandable that the sexual act was regarded as a potential as well as an actual experience, a complicated and, outside of marriage, dangerous undertaking. As second-class citizens, the heroines cannot afford any considerable degree of passion; passion leads to bad marriages.

Austen critics have often been amused at what seems to be the author's relish for seduction-and-pregnancy subplots. Yet since pregnancy was a predictable consequence of engaging in sex, the sexual experience has obviously held an ambivalent place in the imaginations of women throughout civilized history. Freud wrote in *Totem and Taboo* of his curiosity over the primitive tendency of virgins to ward off sex. Perhaps this signifies a tendency to ward off conception and represents a resistance to one's destiny that is analogous to the masculine resistance to replacement by the son. At any rate, in the civil society of Jane Austen only women with the most underdeveloped sense of self and self-preservation view sex exclusively as adventure or flirtation. The girls seduced are always just that — girls — whose ignorance and immaturity render them susceptible. Only a modern critic could see passion in Lydia Bennet, who is infatuated with a uniform, not a man.

Another explanation for the view of sexuality in the novels perhaps is more disturbing. B. C. Southam writes that Jane Austen was aware of the psychological threat of sexuality, "its

melting attack upon the certainties of self-hood and identity."
This tension is evident, Southam shows, in the scene between
Elinor and Willoughby in which "Elinor finds her judgment
endangered by his presence and the physical aspects of his hold
over her are spelt out."[15] For heroines who are struggling for the
certainty of identity and the protective power of selfhood, sexual
passion may be viewed, without apology, as dangerous. And for
individuals who are involved in the rational complexities of
judgment—of immediate judgments that will shape both their
identity and their future—sexual attraction, even when they experience it, may not engage them imaginatively.

Almost every Austen heroine at some point is confronted with a
sexually assertive man, and she either loses interest in him as an
imaginative counterpart (Elizabeth and Wickham, Emma and
Frank Churchill) or rejects him because of a conscious understanding of the danger of his sexuality (Elinor and Willoughby,
Fanny Price and Henry Crawford). It seems that passion is
antithetical to what these heroines are striving for, in the words of
Elizabeth Bennet, as "rational creatures," as women who are
seeking to know themselves and control their lives. In the end they
marry the men who have helped them most in this struggle, who
have been most critical of them and most conscious of their com-
pelling need for honesty.

Jane Austen's awareness of the danger of sexuality implies
neither evasiveness nor prudishness, but a full and brave recognition of what passion meant to the newly emerging "identities" of
the women of her day. Is not the conscious giving up of passion the
price her heroines pay for "consciousness"? Near the end of *Pride
and Prejudice* Jane Austen does not spare her romantic audience
when she writes that the engaged heroine "rather *knew* herself to
be happy, than *felt* herself to be so" (*PP*, p. 372). *Mansfield Park*
contains an unflinching awareness of what sexuality, in the person
of Henry Crawford, means to the precariously growing will of
Fanny Price. Jane Austen knew that passion is too disintegrating a
force to the small degree of selfhood Fanny does possess. (Henry
Crawford knows the same, and pursues her for that very reason.)
Perhaps no other novelist before Virginia Woolf offers a more

harrowing vision of the claims of consciousness for women. One has only to think of the conclusion of *Sense and Sensibility* or the opening chapters of *Persuasion* to see that Austen was fully aware of the potential sickness of consciousness, of the silent, ferocious irony of life *without* passion.

Many aspects of Austen's novels that have come under criticism are better explained with these ideas in view. The seductions, for example, which occur in every novel, have often been viewed as expedient means to forward plot or to explain moral character. Mary Lascelles sees them as an unfortunate but necessary plot convention.[16] But even with regard to plot, seduction is an integral part of the novels in representing the extreme of bad mating. In ironic fiction in which values are submerged and tend to reveal themselves dramatically, an elopement like that of Lydia and Wickham provides a vital boundary in the moral structure of the novel. And through Lydia's behavior we see, and Elizabeth sees, how the defects of one generation survive in the next. Like her mother, Lydia will lead the unconscious life.

The marriages with which every novel ends become far more problematic when seen in this perspective. The traditional attitude that Austen was conforming to the classical comic ending does not take into account the complexity of and the differences among the marriages themselves. We picture Elizabeth at distant Pemberley, attracting other members of her family there, and establishing a new family center. At the conclusion of *Emma,* the hero moves into the heroine's environment and becomes a kind of father to her own father. Emma's marriage contains a shrewd insight into the purposes marriage can serve: in satisfying, for example, the individual's craving to collapse time through incestuous relationships and to make one's world smaller instead of larger. Marriage in Jane Austen is a form of cooperation that has both regressive and progressive tendencies; either way, the personal choice that initiates it is the nexus between the past and the future in the moral life of the individual.

The six novels also reveal historical changes in the institution of marriage, as a comparison of the marriages of Marianne Dashwood and Anne Elliot shows. Through marriage, Marianne finds herself "a wife, the mistress of a family, and the patroness of a village" (*SS*, p. 379) at the Delaford estate. By contrast, Anne Elliot's future is extremely uncertain. She has no estate and no village within which to place herself, and her husband's profession must "pay the tax of quick alarm" (*Per*, p. 252). Like the couple in Arnold's "Dover Beach," Anne and Captain Wentworth have only each other. Not surprisingly, the only successful marriage portrayed in *Persuasion* is the appealing yet surgically locked relationship of the Crofts. The uncertainty of their world demands of them an interdependence and sameness that are almost antithetical to the ideal imagined for Elizabeth and Darcy, Emma and Mr. Knightley.

"Marriage," wrote Dorothy Van Ghent, "that adult initiatory rite that is centrally important in most societies whether barbarous or advanced — is the uppermost concern in *Pride and Prejudice*. As motivation for the story, it is as primatively powerful an urge as is sex in a novel by D. H. Lawrence."[17] Although she identifies this urge as a metaphysical rather than a cultural necessity, Dorothy Van Ghent is unusual in her recognition of the urgency and depth of marriage as an idea in Jane Austen's novels. Walton Litz's attitude is more usual: "The fact is that Jane Austen's world was extremely limited, at least as far as subject matter was concerned, and once she had sighted the basic situations and personalities of that world there was little room for variation in the details of action and setting."[18] I will show, on the contrary, that Austen's novels reveal great contrast and development. Each novel is unique and not necessarily related to the others; each deals with an integrated group of personalities. Surely Catherine Morland and Emma Woodhouse do not, simply because they are both young women, represent the same personality or type; nor is Elizabeth Bennet's situation fundamentally analogous to Anne Elliot's. Mrs. Smith appears in *Persuasion* for reasons very different from those prompting the appearance of Mrs. Jennings in *Sense and Sensibility*. The social distances in the novels are small because internal distances are great: the distance between Elizabeth Bennet and her mother, between Anne Elliot and her father. Jane Austen did not choose to write about the great gulf of class because she wished to expose the less obvious gulf between members of the most homogeneous group, the family, and between members of the same broad social class.

In Jane Austen, personal, domestic experience is a full and valid world—not, as it was to become in George Eliot's fiction, the atomized level to which heroic aspirations eventually sink. In later nineteenth-century novels, marriage, like other experiences of ordinary life, is rarely viewed as an end in itself. It is either the arena of the woman's social ambitions (Becky Sharp, Emma Bovary) or the opportunity for vicarious fulfillment (Dorothea Brooke). Whenever it comes to be desired or perceived as an *actual* experience (Dorothea and Ladislaw) it becomes an *insignificant* experience, part of insignificant middle-class existence. At the close of *Middlemarch,* Dorothea is left with a small circle of admirers as Mrs. Ladislaw; she was more heroic as Casaubon's wife. As soon as Lydgate accepts the actuality of his marriage, his career aspirations plummet and he becomes an ordinary physician. Even David Copperfield's marriage to Agnes seems commonplace compared to his marriage to Dora, which really is commonplace. And one of the reasons Isabel Archer must return to Osmond at the end of *Portrait of a Lady,* rather than stay with Casper Goodwood, is that returning keeps her in the realm of the "terrible" and out of the realm of the ordinary. Isabel is destined to become the portrait of a lady rather than an actual lady. In Jane Austen, the "ordinary" possesses a concrete validity and an intensity of emotions and meaning.

The true moral life of Jane Austen's society has its origins in marriage. Like T. S. Eliot in *The Four Quartets*, Austen might have singled out marriage as the one positive thing, the one institution in life that embodies our hopes for concord, whether or not it realizes them. As the humorously uncharacteristic salute at the close of *Persuasion* suggests, it is not national performances that distinguish human life, but the quality of domestic experience.

The subject of marriage is generic to comedy; and in the comedies of both Shakespeare and Austen we see the biological roots of the genre, the charm against desperation that characterizes the comic view of human existence. Yet the prominence Austen gave to marriage as a subject was not simply a matter of form; it was a social truth. In the society Jane Austen wrote about, marriage truly was the origin of change. For contrary to what is often assumed, the gentry and its lands were highly mobile—marriages made them so.[19] In the early nineteenth century the nexus of social change was to be found in the lower and upper gentry, not in the proletariat or aristocracy.

Every Austen novel testifies to the truth that, in the words of Lawrence Stone, "a class is not a finite group of families, but rather a bus or a hotel, always full but always filled with different people."[20] The great estates of Norland Park and Kellynch Hall change hands in the course of their respective novels, and Mansfield Park witnesses the slow infiltration of the lower-middle-class Price family. *Pride and Prejudice* opens with the news that "Netherfield Park is let at last," to a nouveau riche from the north who Mrs. Bennet hopes will marry one of her daughters. If Mr. Bennet dies before the daughters are married, they will find themselves without a home and accustomed income, in circumstances very similar to those of the Dashwoods at the opening of *Sense and Sensibility*: dependent on the chance liberality of a person of their class with a cottage to rent, if not in even worse straits. The much-emphasized affluence of Jane Austen's characters is precarious indeed. In *Emma,* the well-born Miss Bates has dropped to a barely genteel poverty, while the heroine's governess has risen to be mistress of an estate. The apparent stability of class position in Austen's society was an illusion created by the slowness of change through marriage and "the extraordinary stability of class character, resulting from the chameleon-like adaptability of new families."[21]

Experienced from within, this mobility through marriage took the form of a conflict between marriages of convenience and marriages of feeling. Alliances through marriage were the primary means by which the gentry kept itself afloat. The financial problems of the Mansfield estate make the marriage between Maria Bertram and the stupid Mr. Rushworth "an alliance which [Sir Thomas] could not have relinquished without pain . . . [It was] a marriage which would bring him such an addition of respectability and affluence" (*MP,* p. 201). And on the first page of *Mansfield Park,* Austen shows her awareness of a problem that had existed since the beginning of the seventeenth century—there were more marriageable girls than eligible men.[22]

At the same time, however, forces were at work to counter the system of material alliances. Arranged marriages in England had been under attack for some time.[23] The institution of marriage had changed greatly over the previous two centuries because of the influence of protestant thought. The exaltation of marriage as an honorable state, as one not inferior to celibacy, and the emphasis on companionship that went with this exaltation, led to an increase in young people's freedom to choose their own partners. We witness this change in Austen's novels. Every heroine except Emma Woodhouse must contend with the vergency toward moneyed alliances in her society. At the same time, each heroine is aware of some freedom of personal choice. Young people in Jane Austen are given freedom within a context—say, at a ball. (Indeed, it would seem that balls in Jane Austen are organized for this purpose alone; only the young people dance, while parents and ineligible elders stand by and talk.) Darcy meets Elizabeth Bennet at a ball and begins to fall in love with her; later we learn that he has been intended from his cradle to marry a rich cousin. Yet the novel ends with his marriage to Elizabeth, who, according to Lady Catherine, is "without family, connections, or fortune" (PP, p. 356).

Broadly stated, the structure of Austen's novels records the shift from a tradition-directed to an inner-directed society. There is more to this familiar generalization than may at first appear. The historical changes just mentioned are not merely relevant to Austen's subject. They may indeed account for it and for the fact of her female authorship as well; the effect of these changes on the lives of women in particular was prodigious. This is not to say that the increased freedom of choice in love and marriage did not affect men. Austen shows its effect on Darcy to be profound. Yet that effect is limited by the sheer plurality of his choices and opportunities in life, already there and (because of the increase in male professions) always increasing. The changes in the institution of marriage were, however, to alter the situation of women permanently because they altered women's self-concept. According to Miriam J. Benkovitz, "emotional and sexual self-awareness was the liberating force in woman's self-awareness, her self-evaluation" in the eighteenth century, and was more important than feminist politics in establishing a sense of identity in many women.[24] The increased freedom of choice in marriage led to an emotional awakening in women that was revolutionary; it was the internal force behind the feminist movement of the early nineteenth century and is perhaps the origin of what we understand to be modern womanhood. Moll Flanders, Pamela, Clarissa, Sophia Western, and Austen's early heroines are heroines by virtue of their emotional independence concerning love or marriage, their insistence on freedom of choice in this particular sphere. Elizabeth Bennet's urgency to be accepted as a "rational creature" is not for the sake of reason alone. She makes this claim to Mr. Collins, when he proposes to her and ignores her refusal. She is asserting her own right of choice in sexual decisions, her right to define her own emotional needs, and her right to decide how they shall be satisfied. Heroines of the eighteenth-century novel realize that for their own development and fulfillment, they must first escape the most intimate kind of coercion, the sexual coercion applied through marriage in their society.

Austen's awareness of the ambivalence of these changes is what makes her social analysis so dynamic. In *Mansfield Park,* she portrays the shift from a tradition-directed to an inner-directed society with uncompromising irony. Maria Bertram's marriage to Mr. Rushworth, for example, is not arranged for her, according to tradition; she arranges it herself. In Maria, traditional ambitions have become thoroughly internalized: "It became, by the same rule of moral obligation, her evident duty to marry Mr. Rushworth if she could" (*MP,* pp. 38-39). Society in Jane Austen is not perceived as a vast external framework, like the "social system" alluded to in Dickens's *Dombey and Son,* as much as a subjective structure, a set of biases and beliefs inertly supporting the idea of class distinction in the minds of her characters. In showing the relaxed, materialistic consistency of Maria's mind and the moral inertia of her father's, Austen shows the basic materialism and inertia of the society.

Jane Austen herself was not particularly tradition-directed or conservative, but the society she wrote about was.[25] Her novels do not envision organic, Burkean communities or Penshurst-like estates in which all citizens happily interlock, from high to low; but they do envision a rich society of people who have inherited and internalized this ideal, whatever their practical behavior. Darcy is courteous to his housekeeper and good to his tenants, but to those just a little beneath him socially, to the people of Meryton, he can act as proud and conceited as Lady Catherine de Bourgh. And the snobbery of the middle-class characters is even more contradictory. Austen understood well the self-hatred of the English middle class. The novels are full of middle-class characters, like Mrs. Elton, who after attaining a measure of affluence, want to efface the middle class altogether and pretend they are the members of some ancien régime made up of only the great and the small. Mrs. Elton views Jane Fairfax as a member of the gentle poor, gratefully receiving charity from her patroness, whereas in fact Mrs. Elton's own social origins, education, and future in society are far humbler than Jane's.

Mr. Knightley is Jane Austen's most attractive conservative. If critics had had to depend on Edmund Bertram to argue her conservatism, the dispute over Austen's political vision never would have become lively. But when we read *Emma,* we feel that Mr. Knightley, or what he represents in Highbury, is the best that the English class system could produce in its own defense. As Laurence Lerner has said, Mr. Knightley (and perhaps the novel) is saved from priggishness by his sexual attractiveness.[26] Not attractive only to Emma, he appeals to most of the female characters in the novel. And Mr. Knightley takes a conservative view of most things, most particularly in his lectures to Emma about her social responsibility to those beneath her. In doing so, however, he is primarily taking a realistic view; he understands the conservative nature of society and what can happen to an unintelligent and socially vulnerable person like Harriet Smith (an early Hetty Sorrell) if her expectations are raised to an unreal level and then disappointed. He understands how inorganic the community can be to a Harriet Smith or a Miss Bates. He is a conservative because he is a realist; and his presence in *Emma* is used to show that English society has little place for fancy. This message may seem too harsh for *Emma,* but it clearly is not too harsh for Austen's fiction as a whole. In *Mansfield Park* respectable society is so ruthless that the heroine and hero occupy Mansfield Park as though it were a naval ship, constantly on the alert for attacks from without and disorder from within.

Yet society in Jane Austen is not necessarily evil. Rather, it is a "necessary evil" because as a structure of what Mill called received ideas, it is inert. Our feelings about the moral necessity of inertia for the survival of the human community may decide our feelings about the moral condition of Jane Austen's society. As an artist, Jane Austen resolves the question with a perfectly sustained and relentless dialectic. This dialectic is succinctly expressed in *Mansfield Park.* The heroine's mother, Mrs. Price, marries for love on the first page of the novel and then disappears. She returns to view when Fanny goes back to visit her: "Mrs. Price was not unkind; but instead of gaining in her affection and confidence, and becoming more and more dear, her daughter never met with greater kindness from her than on the first day of her arrival. The instinct of nature was soon satisfied, and Mrs. Price's attachment had no other source" (*MP,* p. 389). Does this passage suggest the weakness of nature and instinct, or the awesome power of society? Does Austen feel that even mother love needs to be encouraged by circumstances, or that circumstances themselves are debilitating to instinct?[27] The cushioned ease of Mansfield Park seems to have utterly neutralized the mother love of Lady Bertram, Mrs. Price's sister. When we read this passage, and others like it in Jane Austen, we are asked to judge instinct and society not as separate forces but as inseparable ones.

In the novels of Jane Austen, "the instinct of nature" is satisfied in society because it exists in society, in the context of family relationships. It is not satisfied in a hypothetical state of nature or even in a natural environment like Box Hill, where, away from the home community, the citizens of Highbury separate into small groups and finally bristle at one another. Such a view is repugnant to many modern readers of Jane Austen, but not necessarily because we are a postromantic generation. Austen's recognition of the value of community in *Emma,* for example, is not altogether inconsistent with romanticism. It is rather a post-Darwinian habit of thought that is to some extent incompatible with Austen's world view: an inclination to ignore what Loren Eiseley has called the "cooperative tendencies" in human culture, or to fail to recognize how these tendencies are related to our struggles. Austen's novels explore the territories of experience in which individuals come together and learn how to survive through cooperation. This process is not perfect; in fact, Jane Austen had early distinguished that world of eternal imperfection and change which was to fascinate Darwin. In her essential views she is closer to her own contemporary, Erasmus Darwin, who in contrast to his grandson emphasized volition, the "striving" of the organism for survival and adjustment. English reaction to the French Revolution swept Erasmus Darwin's ideas out of fashion; and in the end, the silence that enveloped his work was solidified by his grandson's revolutionary emphasis on the struggle for existence in the exterior environment. In *Darwin's Century,* Eiseley interprets this emphasis: "Darwin incorporated into the *Origin of Species* a powerful expression of the utilitarian philosophy of his time. His emphasis lay to a very considerable degree upon selfish motivation, although he admitted that social animals would perpetuate adaptions which benefited the community. On the whole, however, he devoted little attention to the cooperative tendencies in life."[28] Eiseley also draws an interesting connection between Erasmus Darwin and the modern anthropological belief in the intricacy of inner coordination and adjustment in individuals and cultures. "There is an inner cohesiveness which is a product of the social mind," he writes, and which long outlasts the political independence or material technology of a society.[29] In Austen's novels we see the extraordinary articulation of this inner cohesiveness, the drive toward cooperation among individuals and their chameleon-like adaptability to class.

Much modern criticism of Jane Austen reveals the predilection of our age to ignore the interdependence of individual and group life, which is revealed in this drive to adjust and adapt. The historian who in the future must attempt to describe the assumptions of our culture will undoubtedly observe that our notion of self is the polar opposite of our notion of society. Thus, Tony Tanner writes that *Sense and Sensibility* is about "the tension between the potential instability of the individual and the required stabilities of society," as though the stability of Marianne were not "required" in the interests, not of society, but of Marianne herself; as though Elinor's instinct for stability could be viewed as separate from her love for her sister, a love that helps to save Marianne's life.[30] Walton Litz describes Elizabeth Bennet as the "individual will" fighting social restraint (presumably to ally her with nineteenth-century heroines) ignoring her eager self-criticism, her pleasure in social life, and her need for personal happiness and meaning that social life can provide.[31] Instead of seeing the more elusive and problematic drive toward cooperation in the world of the novels, many modern critics have seen the failure of the aggressive spirit of man, the compromise of the will, or the denigration of transcendent yearnings. It is implied that Austen characters possess no striving to coordinate their lives with their environment except what is imposed on them from without. And yet, as Mr. Knightley's reply to Mrs. Elton's suggestion to eat outdoors implies, the "natural" potential in men and women is a civilized one: "My idea of the simple and natural will be to have the table spread in the dining room. The nature and simplicity of gentlemen and ladies" (*E*, p. 355). Readers of Jane Austen often insist that laws, customs, social norms, and preferences are the unexplained assumptions of her world—yet are they? It would seem that Austen's very intent is to illustrate their functions, reveal their strengths and weaknesses, essentially explain or criticize their presence. As Huxley said, it is easy to convince men that they are monkeys. The real effort lies in convincing us that we are men. It is this aspect of humanity that interests Jane Austen: the inscrutable selective wisdom contained in the struggle for existence, the capacity for improvement and the instinct to compromise, the wrestle for harmony within and among individuals.

Irony: The Style

Jane Austen's view of social life is expressed in her narrative style and in the conception of consciousness underlying it. Her irony is the stylistic expression of the dialectical relation between self and society that I have described. Just as the experience of marriage mediates between the individual and society on the level of content, irony mediates between the ideal and the real on the level of form.

Yet if this is true, we may ask, what purpose does the ironic voice serve, if it only epitomizes the novel's action? Why, for example, does not *Pride and Prejudice* open with the dialogue between Mr. and Mrs. Bennet (as Henry James would have it) rather than a disembodied voice of irony, one that stands outside the economy of the plot and undertakes to state directly what is about to be shown?

The answer is that Austen uses a narrator to put forth ideas that, because of their philosophical nature, are beyond the submerged perspective of a character who is actually participating in the society described. Had she wished to present these perceptions through a character, Austen would have needed an outsider, a passive observer like Nick Carraway in *The Great Gatsby,* whose passivity was socially feasible, or who could be allowed to observe without participating. The social life of Long Island in the twenties permitted such observation to a degree that was impossible in Jane Austen's society. In Jane Austen, most social gatherings are so limited in size that even a refusal to participate, such as Darcy's refusal to dance, constitutes an act of participation. It is a mark of the moral weakness of Fitzgerald's story and of the American society he describes that Nick's connection with the Buchanans is never fully acknowledged or understood. The only resolution is escape; and, at the close of the novel, Nick goes back to the Midwest. In Jane Austen's society, there is no confidence in the freedom to depart, above all for women; as a result, one's connection to a particular social group is an assumed and active thing. Thus a truly philosophical detachment is impossible for the submerged character. And most of the "philosophers" in Jane Austen are either fools (Mary Bennet) or failures (her father). Mr. Knightley is an interesting exception, yet even his wisdom is chastised by Emma's vitality and by his love for that vitality.[32]

The only vent for philosophically oriented commentary, then, must be found in a narrative voice, which is free of social constraints as no character can be. But the substance of this commentary is of course directly related to the concerns of the plot and meant to be applied there. The opening line of *Pride and Prejudice*, for example, is the beginning of a chain reaction in irony; the line reverberates throughout the entire first chapter, indeed the entire novel, and derives its brilliance from that reverberation. But let us consider a seemingly more autonomous instance of the narrator's irony: "Human nature is so well disposed towards those who are in interesting situations, that a young person, who either marries or dies, is sure of being kindly spoken of" (*E*, p. 181). The epigrammatic clarity of the statement almost raises it out of the novel and its concerns; it seems gratuitously playful and offhand. Yet like Oscar Wilde's humor, Jane Austen's humor in this instance is outrageous and meaningful because it *is* offhand, because it contains an offhand dismissal of death as an "interesting situation." To the extent that this dismissal shocks and delights the reader, it is part of the narrative economy. And its meaning is very much a part of *Emma*, which is itself a comedy about "human nature." It is a cardinal rule of comedy that no one dies; on the most amusing level the statement says that only in comedy, or in Highbury, can death be viewed as an interesting situation. And yet if we take the statement more seriously we learn more from it. The cosmic intuition of Jane Austen's comedy contains a very deep conviction of the irrelevance of death. There has always seemed to me a boldness in her absolute lack of interest in death as an event in itself. Austen is unusual in this indifference; as Lionel Trilling has said, no subject recurs more often in literature than death, and it is the tendency of most literature "to soften death's aspect by showing it as through a veil, or by asking us to 'accept' it as a part of life."[33] Through death in literature, as Freud has said, the reader experiences a vicarious death and yet survives it. He discovers the plurality of lives for which he longs; and he sees people who know how to die. The unimaginable is made imaginable for his benefit. Death becomes part of life, part of the rationality or irrationality of being alive.

In no way does Jane Austen construe death to be a part of life. The human response to death *is* a part of life, a part that she examines comically in *Emma*, through Mrs. Churchill's death, and satirically in *Persuasion*, through Dick Musgrove and Fanny Harville's deaths. In her response to death she shows (through irony) that death itself is unimaginable, irrelevant, and absurd; to attempt to incorporate it into living experience, as Mrs. Musgrove and Highbury do, is to evade it, to pretend that it can be tamed and "kindly spoken of." The great humor of the statement from *Emma* lies in the evasion of death that it implies; its humor opens the reader to its wisdom, which is the tolerance of the evasion. Like Emma herself, "human nature" is full of evasion and cruelty and yet perpetually deserving.

That there is an element of cruelty in Jane Austen's irony and in the quotation from *Emma* just cited cannot be denied. The neighborhood is as blind to the living, those who marry, as it is to the dead. It is through cruelty that the comic author earns his compassion or tolerance. In one of the few references to political events in her letters, Austen writes of the bloody battle of Albuera; "How horrible it is to have so many people killed! — And what a blessing that one cares for none of them!"[34] I can think of no better instance of the sheer despotism of Jane Austen's irony than this horrifying and true statement. Often read too simply as the expression of cold-hearted indifference, the statement holds up an intolerable truth: the poverty of our imaginations saves us from the recollection of our common humanity. Jane Austen had Montaigne's sense that human reason is a double-edged sword. Her irony can always be read in several ways, her voice heard in several tones. The quoted statement says both that it is *not* a blessing and that it *is* a blessing that one cares for none of the dead soldiers. The tone is both cold-hearted *and* passionate. Both sentiments and tones are equally sincere and valid.

One of the larger functions of irony as a method of comprehension is that it allows a respect for amoral diversity (we could say society or reality) to coexist with a fidelity to morality (the claims of the self or the ideal). Unkindness, smugness, and snobbery are all systematically condemned in the novels, yet the individuals who possess these faults in excess are neither rejected nor deflated, both because the good persons in the novels do not possess the smugness to reject them, and because the author's imaginative integrity will not allow their deflation. In Jane Austen, morality is the regulator of life, not its oppressor. The moral vision of *Pride and Prejudice* regulates Mrs. Bennet, Lydia, and Mr. Collins, for example, without compromising their audacity; morality and "reality" are held together through irony. "Mr. Collins had only to change from Jane to Elizabeth — and it was soon done — done while Mrs. Bennet was stirring the fire" (*PP*, p. 71). This statement constitutes a moral observation of Mr. Collins without depreciating his absurdity. The same may be said of Austen's use of understatement. "Mr. Collins was not a sensible man" (*PP*, p. 70). To say that Mr. Collins is a fool is certainly true but in essence accusatory. To say that he is not sensible introduces a standard of character that he fails to achieve but that is nevertheless accessible. It is a way of acknowledging his defects without devaluing him. Irony is the bond between what is and what should be; it allows them to coexist without negating one another.

It may be misleading to refer to "what is" in Jane Austen as "reality," because the modern definition of reality is whatever is hard, gross, or unpleasant; it is the "reality principle" that renounces pleasure. One of the pejorative opposites of our idea of reality is, I think, the imagination. The imagination is seen to be at odds with reality; when a reviewer refers to a writer as "a very imaginative writer," he usually means a subjective or fanciful writer. Saint-Exupery is pejoratively called an "imaginative writer," and children's literature is often called imaginative because it is ostensibly at odds with adult reality. Even when the pejorative connotation of imagination does not apply, we still perceive a schism between imagination and reality, like the schism we perceive between the self and society. Various modern writers from Virginia Woolf to Wallace Stevens view the artist as a mediator between imagination and reality.

In Jane Austen the diversity of "reality" is so extensive and

interesting as to constitute an imaginative triumph. There is no
schism between imagination and reality in the novels except what
the deluded individual may see there. Catherine Morland first
learns that the gothic imagination exaggerates reality, and then
that reality is as inventive and surprising as any enthusiast of fiction could wish. Elizabeth Bennet was Jane Austen's favorite heroine, possible because, like herself, Elizabeth delighted in the diversity and changefulness of reality. Yet this delight needs regulation.
In Austen's novels, morality regulates the imagination without
suppressing it, just as social structures can regulate the self without suppressing it. The moral vision of *Emma* structures its exuberance, just as Mr. Knightley regulates Emma without repressing
her spirit. Indeed Emma's wit is vitalized by his presence, just as
the novel's exuberance gains swiftness and power in the moral
context. Within an ironic method of comprehension, the moral
and imaginative faculties can coexist. In nonironic works, like
Dickens's early novels, coexistence is almost impossible without
injury to at least one faculty. The imaginative vision of *Oliver
Twist* is ingenious; the moral vision is static. Through irony, morality and the imagination may be defined jointly; in Jane Austen
they become interdependent faculties.

I stress the centrality of Austen's irony to her moral vision
because readers and critics alike tend to ignore it. Most studies of
Austen's style, for example, base their conclusions on a preference
for one strain in the narrator's diction: C. S. Lewis cites the Johnsonian, Mark Schorer the mercantile strain.[35] Graham Hough's
complex study of *Emma* asserts that the objective narrative with
its Johnsonian vocabulary sets "the standard by which all the rest is
measured," and that "the characters we approve assimilate their
speech to the objective narrative." Those who assimilate to the
objective narrative most completely, such as Mr. Knightley, are
the highest on an unequivocal moral scale. Hough concludes that
the narrative structure of Austen's novels reveals a static and anachronistic conception of her world; that she "returns us to the
ethos of the Rambler."[36]

The trouble with this view is that in fact there is no "objective
narrative" in the novels who presents ideas to us in a Johnsonian

way, "uncoloured, not from any particular point of view, manifestly to be accepted as true."[37] The opening description of Emma, which Hough gives as an example of objective narrative, is full of irony, taking as it does Emma's own spoiled view of herself: "Emma Woodhouse, handsome, clever, and rich, with a comfortable home and happy disposition, seemed to unite some of the best blessings of existence; and had lived nearly twenty-one years in the world with very little to distress or vex her" (E, p. 5). These lines say to us much more than that Emma is handsome, clever, and rich—if that were all that was intended the novel could not have progressed. Like the opening of *Anna Karenina*, the statement is made ironic by the fact that several hundred pages follow it. The statement tells us that we are about to read how this young woman comes to be distressed and vexed; just as the opening of Tolstoy's novel tells us that we are about to read about an unhappy family that is unhappy in its own unique and complicated way. The opening sentence of *Emma* is one of the most direct and uncomplicated statements in all of Jane Austen, and yet it contains this extensive irony. In her "objective narrative" style, Austen is Voltaire's counterpart. Just as Voltaire's clear, short sentences with their clear, simple concepts and vocabulary suggest the stylistic model for the academic rationalist, the lucid, Johnsonian cadence of Austen's objective narrative suggests the model for moral rationalism. But both are misleading models. For without Voltaire's polemical intention and Austen's ironical intention, their styles would be flat and would be poor vehicles for communicating ideas.

An emphasis on one strain in Austen's diction also discounts her dramatic irony. Mr. Knightley's speech, for example, is surely the highest on an unequivocal moral scale, if an unequivocal moral scale exists in *Emma*. He is Johnsonian in his wisdom and anachronistic in his views. Yet Emma, whom the novel (and Mr. Knightley) essentially praise, is neither. This is an example of dramatic irony on a large scale. Whether narrative or dramatic, Austen's irony is more integral to her vision than any particular diction.

Austen creates another irony by means of the juxtaposition of

narrative and dialogue. Take for example the first description of
Mrs. Bennet, following the opening dialogue of *Pride and
Prejudice*: "(Mrs. Bennet) was a woman of mean understanding,
little information, and uncertain temper. When she was discontented she fancied herself nervous. The business of her life was to
get her daughters married; its solace was visiting and news" *PP,* p.
5). Taken out of context, this description sounds objectively true,
Johnsonian, and clear. Yet when juxtaposed with the character of
Mrs. Bennet, whom we have just heard in dialogue, the description seems deficient, if only because it *is* description; and it
pertains more to Mr. Bennet's view of his wife than to the
narrator's. After the superb irony of the opening dialogue, direct
description is above all disconcerting. We wish to interpret the
lines because they have surprised us; and for that reason our interpretations are arbitrary, designed to alleviate bafflement rather
than penetrate it. To some, the lines seem ironic because they *are*
direct; to others, like Hough, they seem objective because they
stand out against the subjectivity of the dialogue. The larger issue,
however, relates more to the lines' effect than to their meaning.
Directness in the context of irony is as baffling as irony in the
context of directness. No single interpretation of the lines'
meaning will be universally acknowledged; the only truth is the
mutiplicity of truth, or the uncertainty of truth, or the presence of
ceaseless surprise.

The example from *Pride and Prejudice* is more clear-cut than
most; we always know who is speaking when we read it, whether
Mr. Bennet, his wife, or the narrator. Yet Austen does not keep to
one point of view with Jamesian scrupulosity. Her narrative often
shades into a free, indirect style, or a style deeply colored by the
point of view of a particular character. The modulations and
shadings imbue the narrative with an uncertainty and irony that
are essential to its grasp upon the reader's mind. Take for example
this passage from *Emma*, the first description of Harriet Smith:

> She was a very pretty girl, and her beauty happened to be of a
> sort which Emma particularly admired. She was short,
> plump and fair, with a fine bloom, blue eyes, light hair,

regular features, and a look of great sweetness; and before the end of the evening, Emma was as much pleased with her manners as her person, and quite determined to continue the acquaintance.

She was not struck by anything remarkably clever in Miss Smith's conversation, but she found her altogether very engaging — not inconveniently shy, not unwilling to talk — and yet so far from pushing, shewing so proper a deference, seeming so pleasantly grateful for being admitted to Hartfield, and so artlessly impressed by the appearance of every thing in so superior a style to what she had been used to, that she must have good sense and deserve encouragement. Encouragement should be given. Those soft blue eyes and all those natural graces should not be wasted on the inferior style of Highbury and its connections. The acquaintance she had already formed were unworthy of her. The friends from whom she had just parted, though very good sort of people, must be doing her harm . . . [They] must be coarse and unpolished, and very unfit to be the intimates of a girl who wanted only a little more knowledge and elegance to be quite perfect. She would notice her; she would improve her; she would detach her from her bad acquaintance, and introduce her into good society; she would form her opinions and manners. It would be an interesting, and certainly a very kind undertaking; highly becoming to her own situation in life, her leisure, and powers. (*E,* p. 24)

The passage begins in impersonal "objective" narrative and ends in narrative that is deeply colored by Emma's point of view; it is a stylistic expression, in other words, of the interdependence of inner and outer experience that characterizes the novel's content. The brilliance of the piece lies in the gradual modulation: when do we stop believing what we are reading? When do we begin to distrust Emma? There is no particular word or sentence that stops us; in fact, the strength of the passage, and of the portrait of Emma as a whole, is that we are not allowed to be that conclusive about her. We never stop trusting her completely; indeed we do not dare. The narrative is too restless for judgment. No sooner have we criticized Emma for her condescending attitude toward

Harriet than we are confronted with Harriet's subservient gratitude: "Miss Woodhouse had . . . actually shaken hands with her at last!" (*E*, p. 25). Can we judge one without the other, or should we, like Emma, make Harriet less responsible? No sooner have we renounced Emma's snobbery toward the Coles—"Nothing should tempt *her* to go . . . and she regretted that her father's known habits would be giving her refusal less meaning than she could wish" (*E*, p. 207)—than we realize that she actually wants to go, that in fact she has no objection to being with the Coles, only to the *idea* of being with them.

Consider another example from *Persuasion:* "He had been most warmly attached to her, and had never seen a woman since whom he thought her equal; but, except from some natural sensation of curiosity, he had no desire of meeting her again. Her power with him was gone for ever. It was now his object to marry" (*Per*, p. 61). This passage is interior monologue and contains Captain Wentworth's evasion of his feeling for Anne. Yet few readers are aware of this on first reading because Wentworth's decisive, penetrating style is somewhat similar to that of the objective narrator. The ambiguity is useful and intended, for it is our doubt of his willingness to love Anne again that makes their reconciliation so interesting and exciting. The statement, "it was now his object to marry," is both objectively true and subjectively uttered, and the blur between objective and subjective thought is intended, as in the *Emma* passage. Wentworth and Anne's future depends on the extent to which he *believes* he is being objective and truthful when he says that her power with him is gone forever and that it is now his object to marry. Wayne Booth believes that this dipping in and out of the character's mind is too arbitrary and tends to contaminate the realism of the action. He reveals in this judgment the modern reverence for "experience"; and he overlooks the fact that part of the novel's meaning, and much of the reader's experience in reading it, lies in this modulation of inner and outer perspectives, the continuous variation of distance and angle.

The multiple voices in Austen's fiction, then, make up not a simple, static moral scale, but a complex, dynamic one. The voice of Austen's fiction is unsteady, pliable, or in the words of Mary

Lascelles, "chameleon-like": "[It] varies in colour as the habits of expression of the several characters impress themselves on the relation of the episodes in which they are involved, and on the description of their situations."[38] The rich and heavy narration of the arrival of the Bertrams' party in the midst of the solemn grandeur of Sotherton is an example: "Mr. Rushworth was at the door to receive his fair lady, and the whole party were welcomed by him with due attention. In the drawing-room they were met with equal cordiality by the mother, and Miss Bertram had all the distinction with each that she could wish. After the business of arriving was over, it was first necessary to eat, and the doors were thrown open to admit them through one or two intermediate rooms into the appointed dining parlour, where a collation was prepared with abundance and elegance" (*MP,* p. 84). One could almost say that in the above passage Sotherton is speaking, or perhaps the event itself is speaking, the group consciousness that makes itself felt during an event. This voice gradually expands to include Mrs. Rushworth's relation, modulates to an interior monologue of Fanny's, and finally shifts into dialogue. The shifting and alteration of point of view, characteristic of all the novels, gives us the impression that experience is endlessly discoverable. Elizabeth comes to know Darcy with a similar multiplicity of view: through his manners, his letter, the appearance of his estate, the report of his housekeeper, his portrait, and finally his own self-analysis. Her knowledge is never complete, and neither is his.

Austen's various narrators perpetuate the fertile ambiguity and uncertainty of the work itself and are indispensable to it. George Eliot's narrators conform more to Hough's definition; her disinterested and compassionate narrative voice stands outside the economy of the narrative for the purpose of complementing and enfolding the story with its wisdom, and this voice is entirely stable and trustworthy. Austen's method is closer to that of Henry James; James also makes use of coloured narrative, free, indirect style, and narrative irony, yet his narrative variability is far more certain and directed than Austen's. "We never know quite where we are with Jane Austen," writes John Bayley, "as we know where we are with George Eliot, and even Henry James. *He* may sometimes not have been quite sure what he thought about things, but then we can see him being not quite sure—Jane Austen's certainties are much more enigmatic."[39] Unlike James, Austen's narrative variations seem to increase knowledge by default; they assume the unknowability of experience. James's variations are deliberately intended to increase knowledge and to arrive at knowledge. This progress in knowledge and intimacy gives the reader a handle on the story from its outset—a security of purpose, an awareness of accumulating knowledge. We never feel this security in Jane Austen; her very purpose is to deprive the reader of purpose, to undermine any secure viewpoint or state of mind that would structure his experience of the story and allow him to transcend it. The narrative dips in and out, shifts from plane to plane, grasping and then releasing a particular consciousness: authorial, individual, family, neighborhood, even, as Mary Lascelles has shown, the collective consciousness that forms spontaneously around an event. Such a narrative mode reveals an intuition of life that is inconclusive, restless, alive—the opposite of Mr. Knightley's or Edmund Bertram's organized wisdom.

The initial effect of this narrative pliability, then, is to interfere with a static, and of course a dogmatic, viewpoint. The opening of *Pride and Prejudice* passes from the universal, absolute declaration to the localized incident that challenges it; in a pattern characteristic of Jane Austen, values and perceptions are asserted and then tacitly challenged. The narrative, with its innumerable planes of consciousness, is ceaselessly overcoming itself, and implies a structure that is the opposite of transcendent complacency and a resistance to it. Over and over, the narrative voice thwarts a particular character's tendency—finally, the reader's tendency—to simplify his world in order to live in it, to regard conclusions that have only temporary validity as permanent. No one viewpoint is adequate or conclusive; the experience of spontaneous movement from one plane of awareness to the next is the essence of the moral life of the novels, and of Jane Austen's wisdom.

In the world of Austen's novels, birth, death, passion, and God do not exist as transcendent realities. They are enclosed in human time and filtered through opinion; they appear in their truncated form among the details that make up the day-to-day life of the novels. And because of the ceaseless intimacies and transformations of the narrative, no level of consciousness is secure or consistent enough to allow us to distance ourselves from the commonplace happenings of the story; we are forced to comprehend the preoccupations of common life. We receive the unalloyed burden of the present. And the absence of metaphor in the novels intensifies our consciousness of the present's unavoidable responsibilities: family, married, and communal relations. There is no transcendence without including the burden of the present in some way.

In spite of the mundane concerns, the absence of props and physical description in the novels lends them a heightened, cerebral quality, as if no distractions are allowed, no lapses into wadded unawareness. The dismissal of the unrealities people prefer is relentless and bracing. And when we consider that this unrelieved attention attaches itself to the present, to day-to-day existence, we can understand why irony was the only mode proper to the handling of Austen's subject. How can the present be conceived without ambivalence? As Northrop Frye has said, in irony the wheel of time completely encloses the action, and there is no sense of an original contact with a relatively timeless world. When we finish reading a work of ironic comedy, deserts of futility open up on all sides, and we may have, in spite of the humor, a sense of nightmare and a close proximity to something demonic.[40]

Paradoxically, the unsteadiness of Austen's narrative is not corrosive but cohesive. This is perhaps the greatest achievement of the ironic method of comprehension: it surveys the ever changing landscape of consciousness with equanimity: it is passive yet binding. Until *Persuasion* it disavows a "center of consciousness" because, to Jane Austen, the individual consciousness cannot be separated from the world; and the family consciousness, neighborhood consciousness, and even the consciousness that collects during an event are realized in the individual at different moments. All planes intersect, overlap, and blend in various ways; the individual consciousness is pliable, indefinite, expansive, decaying, and capable of change. And as I have suggested, this intuition of the malleability of individual beings and the potential cohesiveness of their experience is realized in the subject matter of the novels, which is marriage, the nexus of generational change.

Ironic Comedy and Satiric Realism: The Two Structures

It has been said that satire shows people stealing and comedy shows people trying to steal. Like Shakespeare's Malvolio, comic villains do not succeed; and their efforts, like the steward's efforts to marry Olivia or Mr. Collins's proposal to Elizabeth, become part of the irresistible comedy of existence. In satire, on the other hand, actions occur that seem to imply an unwelcome, even a tragic, outcome; and our amusement is like the laughter of an audience for *Measure for Measure;* it takes on the more worried tones of feeling. If the ethos of comedy is an ethos of pleasure, the ethos of satire, as in Swift's "Voyage to the Houyhnhnms" or *Mansfield Park,* is one of disappointment or pain.

The novels of Jane Austen may be grouped according to this distinction: the three works of ironic comedy, *Northanger Abbey, Pride and Prejudice,* and *Emma;* and the three works of satiric realism, *Sense and Sensibility, Mansfield Park,* and *Persuasion.* Austen was attracted to both strains and alternated between them; within each novel the tension is often felt, and a minor character or subplot in the first group may resemble foreground material in the second. Eleanor Tilney, for example, is an early Anne Elliot: motherless, despondent, and subject to an insensitive and egotistical father. Mr. Bennet is a comic character until his daughter Lydia runs off with Wickham, when his carelessness as a parent is realized in the carelessness of his daughter. He slips out of satire and back into comedy when Lydia is married and Jane and Elizabeth are spared social humiliation.

In *Northanger Abbey, Pride and Prejudice,* and *Emma,* the heroines come close to danger for a brief moment—Mrs. Bennet almost destroys the marriage chances of her daughters—but safety and happiness burst in at the end. These novels provide a carefully closed system which makes resilience possible. And a belief in resilience is essential to comedy: Catherine Morland survives her humiliating expulsion from Northanger without being "essentially hurt by it" (*NA*, p. 252); Elizabeth is wiser and happier for having criticized herself; and Emma, at the very least, is better off in the end than when she started. Consciousness is good; self-knowledge leads to happiness; and the mood of these novels is one of acceptance. The real test for all the heroines is learning to accept the world as they find it; yet in the ironic comedies, the misery of this realization is short-lived. The moment of self-awareness is frightening but brief. No sooner has Emma faced the terrible loneliness of a future without Mr. Knightley than he proposes to her.

In the works of satiric realism, as in so many nineteenth-century novels, the miseries of actuality are felt from the outset and examined unflinchingly. In *Sense and Sensibility* the opening scene between Mr. and Mrs. John Dashwood portrays a polite form of stealing; comic barriers are penetrated and chaos is breaking in on all sides; actions occur and people are hurt. An impractical widow finds herself homeless and without an accustomed income (*Sense and Sensibility*); a meddling aunt uproots a young child from her family (*Mansfield Park*); an older woman persuades a young woman to refuse the man she loves (*Persuasion*). And although all three works end happily, the degree of enlightenment and the nature of happiness are questionable. The mood is one of fatigue, not resilience. Marianne will never be the same; Fanny will always be the same; the eight years of Anne Elliot's estrangement from Captain Wentworth cannot be made up.

Let us consider the more factual contrasts between the two groups. Reflecting the social situation of the eighteenth century, the ironic comedies have a relatively small social setting; geographical distances seem short and the number of characters is relatively limited. The social setting is secure; the heroes (Tilney, Darcy, and Knightley) are superior in wealth and status to the heroines, and each hero owns an estate that is emblematic of his solidity and worth. (Darcy's Pemberley has a good library.) The progress of the heroine's education or enlightenment is the major concern of the plot, and this progress is essentially direct. Consistent with the cosmic intuition of comedy, the mood, language, and treatment of incident give these novels a timeless and even spaceless quality. The opening pages of each ironic comedy do not specify time and place except as "day" and "neighborhood"; the result is a sense of expansion. As I will show in later chapters, *Pride and Prejudice* and *Emma* succeed in resisting time through an assertion of the present.

In the nineteenth-century world of satiric realism we have a greater sense of geographical distance, of people belonging to certain places and of those places possessing a particular ethos. The ethos of London is powerfully felt in both *Sense and Sensibility* and *Mansfield Park*; in *Persuasion,* the problem of the separation of places and of the unsuspected psychic distances between them is a major concern: "Anne had not wanted this visit to Uppercross, to learn that a removal from one set of people to another, though at a distance of only three miles, will often include a total change of conversation, opinion and idea . . . It was highly incumbent on her to clothe her imagination, her memory and all her ideas in as much of Uppercross as possible" (*Per,* pp. 42-43). We find in these works a greater number of characters and an increase in the number of families examined; as a result, the interrelationships become more complicated. More traveling takes place, and a major change of location occurs in each: the Dashwoods move from Sussex to Devonshire; Fanny Price is taken from her seaport home to a large country estate; the Elliots move to Bath. The mood of uncertainty and uprootedness that results from these changes of home is intensified by the fact that the hero in each novel has no secure estate. Willoughby, Edward Ferrars, Edmund Bertram, and the young Wentworth are all financially unstable at the time when it is most crucial to the heroine that they not be.

The moral action of these novels moves at great cost toward integration and cooperation. The threat of disintegration is real, and the characters are almost wrenched into the final state of cooperation. The sense of disintegration also accounts for a different perception of time in these novels, which, like that of later novels in the nineteenth century, is heavily historical, not the light, dazzling surface of the present in comedy. Each satiric novel opens with a description of the history of a family. *Persuasion* is remarkable for the evocation of time past in its opening chapters:

> Thirteen years had seen her mistress of Kellynch Hall, presiding and directing with a self-possession and decision which could never have given the idea of her being younger than she was. For thirteen years had she been doing the honours, and laying down the domestic law at home, and leading the way to the chaise and four, and walking immediately after Lady Russell out of all the drawing-rooms and dining-rooms in the country. Thirteen winters' revolving frosts had seen her opening every ball of credit which a scanty neighborhood afforded; and thirteen springs shewn their blossoms, as she travelled up to London with her father, for a few weeks annual enjoyment of the great world. (*Per,* pp. 6-7)

Space is also more sharply defined in these novels; we have a strong, heavy sense of the large, enclosed spaces of Norland, Mansfield, and Kellynch, and a contrasting sense of the small rooms of Barton Cottage, the cramped and confined living quarters of the Price family at Portsmouth and of Mrs. Smith at Bath. It accords with this sense of defined space that the heroines in these works do not experience the unequivocal breakthrough in self-awareness that Catherine, Elizabeth, and Emma experience. Marianne moves from sensibility to sense, from one ideology to another; Anne Elliot moves from self-abnegation to self-justification. Consciousness is painful, and self-awareness does not necessarily lead to happiness. Anne, an almost fully conscious heroine from the beginning, is unhappy until the last chapter of *Persuasion.* Fanny's painful, sensitive consciousness is one of the most alluring aspects of *Mansfield Park.*

Each of the comic novels, *Northanger Abbey, Pride and Prejudice,* and *Emma,* centers on one youthful and vivacious heroine. The structures of the satiric works accommodate themselves to two heroines: the young Anne Elliot and the older Anne Elliot, Elinor and Marianne, Fanny and Mary Crawford. Each of these novels deals with the tension of opposing views of life; in *Persuasion,* the opposing forces are dramatized in a single person. The young Anne Elliot is the rational and reflective chooser whom Elizabeth Bennet becomes; the older Anne Elliot possesses a romantic sensibility as acute as that of Fanny or Marianne.

The difference in heroines brings up perhaps the most essential difference between the two modes. In the works of ironic comedy, the action progresses toward cognitive enlightenment; once the heroine is enlightened, she is capable of love and the story ends. Catherine, Elizabeth, and Emma are just beginning to love their future husbands, or to know that they love them, when the novels close. They will love their husbands, of this we feel certain, because they know them and want to love them. What is important at the close of the novels is that they are capable of love: "Elizabeth . . . rather *knew* that she was happy, than *felt* herself to be so (*PP*, p. 372). Elizabeth's change is a matter of the mind, of knowing, more than of heart. To put it another way, her change of mind brings about a change of heart. And the basic interest and suspense in each of these novels is epistemological: Will Catherine's eyes ever open? Will Elizabeth learn to be fair? Will Emma ever see straight? Reminiscent of the metaphysical frame of earlier fiction, these novels are structured according to a platonic awakening. As a result, the hero figures as a kind of Virgilian guide who leads the heroine to truth. (Tilney and Knightley are the archetypal teacher-heroes.) The philosophical problem that informs these novels, then, is the relationship between cognition and action: the heroine must learn to see clearly enough to choose the correct course of action.

Since the world of ironic comedy is one of unfathomable expansion, this emphasis upon comprehension is inevitable. In the opening chapter of *Pride and Prejudice,* the voices of Mr. and Mrs. Bennet drift in space, disembodied, moving (in the words of Mary Ellmann) to the rhythms of miscomprehension. The narrative voice attempts to pin down the corners of this floating world; the preeminent necessity for both narrator and character is cognition. This world is too fluid for passion to take form within it; it offers too little resistance. Cognition alone provides protection against irrationality.

In ironic comedy, the individuals are too large for the institutions in which they participate. The entail in *Pride and Prejudice,* for example, is an instance of overt economic discrimination against women, yet it becomes engulfed in the presence of its absurd representative, Mr. Collins. The world collapses into the mind; and so the strengthened, disciplined mind becomes the only salvation. Emma's *heart* is in the right place all along; she wants to go to the Coles' dinner, and she does not at all enjoy snubbing the Martins. It is a failure of sight, of mind, that leads her astray, a mind undisciplined and run away with itself. Austen's emphasis upon a mind in excess of the world, upon the mind's tyranny, reappears a century later in Woolf, Joyce, and the later Henry James.

In the works of satiric realism the weight of the action finally falls not on cognitive enlightenment but on disillusionment; enlightenment always takes the form of loss. Marianne must lose Willoughby for the sake of truth; Fanny must lose the cherished image of her home and mother for the sake of growth; Anne Elliot must lose eight years to learn that the original impulses of her heart were right. And the disillusionment, like the novels' general concern, is more a matter of heart than of mind. The center of interest, the reservoir of hope and curiosity in these novels, is feeling rather than knowing: What will become of Marianne's passion, of Fanny's tenderness, of Anne's loneliness? As a result, the heroes of these novels are not involved in leading the heroines to emotional intelligence but are actually part of the disillusionment. Willoughby is a cad; Edward Ferrars foolishly engages himself to the wrong girl; Edmund is temporarily captivated by the wrong woman; and even Captain Wentworth stays angry years longer than he admits he should have. The ethical problem in this mode is establishing a connection between feeling and acting. Fanny probes continually: How much of what I feel to be right can I perform? And the obstacles to right action are emotional and psychological, not epistemological.

All three of the works of satiric realism explore passion with considerable depth and honesty, and as Austen's treatment of it evolves, we witness a kind of Freudian progression. Marianne's passion for Willoughby is narcissistic, an extension of her self-love, and, by implication, autoerotic. In *Mansfield Park,* Fanny loves her "brother" Edmund from childhood with an unrelieved passional intensity. But in her last novel Austen for the first time explored an adult passion, the love between equal yet opposite personalities — one of the few instances of it, as a matter of fact, in English fiction.

The works of satiric realism lead immediately to the nineteenth-century novel, to the fiction of Charlotte Brontë, Dickens, and Eliot. In Jane Austen, the world of satiric realism is vengeful and real, a fixed social environment full of obstacles and repressions for the individual who lives in it. Unlike the inexplicable world of comic exuberance, this world is familiar and historical; instead of eluding the individual, it overpowers him. These novels are similar to nineteenth-century fiction in viewing the individual against a larger social background, like a Hardy character against the Wessex landscape. The background is dense and unyielding, and so passion forms naturally within it, as a resistance to it. The social world of *Sense and Sensibility* and the passion of Marianne belong to one another, just as Anna Karenina's passion belongs to the rigid society of Tolstoy's novel. The world of *Jane Eyre* must be stiff and oppressive in order to produce and sustain the ferocious passion of its heroine. For all Charlotte Brontë's disdain for an author to whom "the passions are perfectly unknown," she followed unawares in Austen's train.

The emphasis on mind in the works of ironic comedy involves a subtle yet definite undervaluing of the heart. All the heroines are capable of love but do not love within the limits of the story. Their love is cognitive love; Elizabeth loves with her mind. It is an indication of Jane Austen's slightly horrifying honesty that she does not present Elizabeth's love as more than that. Perhaps this explains the slightly brittle tone of *Pride and Prejudice,* a quality that continues to make itself felt after several readings. Not until *Persuasion* does Jane Austen portray a woman who loves both intelligently and passionately, and that is only after she has rejected the first impulses of her heart. In *Pride and Prejudice,* and more emphatically in *Emma,* the love relationship is seen as a relationship of minds; marriage is the entrusted proximity of those minds. Catherine Morland's "learning" experience is transformed in *Emma* to a matter of sheer contact with the "other." It is as if simply by encountering one another Emma and Mr. Knightley influence one another and do one another good.

If Elizabeth loves with her mind, Fanny Price thinks with her heart. And the emphasis on emotion in the works of satiric realism ultimately involves a compromise of perception, particularly with regard to the heroine's level of awareness at the end of the story. The opposing critical attitudes toward Fanny Price may perhaps be resolved here. There are two fundamental opinions of her: first, that she is admirable because she feels deeply and worries about what is right and wrong; and second, that she is objectionable because she deceives herself. I suggest that both opinions are valid. Fanny's heavy emotionalism and the guilt that arises from her self-scrutiny prevent her from admitting to moral weaknesses (her jealousy of Mary Crawford, for example) that her conscience would abhor: "Without any particular affection for her eldest cousin, her tenderness of heart made her feel that she could not spare him" (*MP*, p. 428). Fanny's "tenderness" disguises her apathy — even from herself. As in the other novels of this mode, dealing with and resolving matters of the heart involves a compromise of the intellect. Marianne's life with Colonel Brandon and Edmund's life with Fanny include the closing off of certain possibilities, the shutting out of perceptions that are opposed to the irrevocable facts of the present. Only when she has gained Wentworth's love once more is Anne Elliot fully conscious of what she almost lost (so conscious that she is physically overpowered); because admitting that she might have lost it through her own choice is intolerable, the possibility is shut out. She was right to refuse him, she says, she was right to submit to Lady Russell. In each of the works of satiric realism, certain admissions are unbearable. What might have been — marriage to a person one loved, or permanent self-imposed estrangement from that person — becomes one more subject for detached observation, as what might be. To Marianne Dashwood and Edmund Bertram, marriage becomes vengefully simple. One learns to think only of what is, not of what might have been. One lives by irony and sentiment; one observes convention.

The novels of satiric realism are not without a sense of nightmare; they anticipate the nineteenth-century novel in their awareness of the tragic potential of everyday life. In *Sense and Sensibility,* Jane Austen rejects an old notion of tragedy for a new one.

People do not die of unrequited love, the author suggests; that only happens in literature. Yet they may do worse: they may survive and lower their expectations. "They had in fact nothing to wish for, but the marriage of Colonel Brandon and Marianne, and rather better pasturage for their cows" (*SS,* pp. 374-375). Yet behind this irony lies another more stringent irony, one not found in later novelists like Charlotte Brontë and George Eliot; and that is the knowledge that to prefer tragedy to the living is an unspeakable luxury. Marianne *is* better alive and married to Colonel Brandon than dead. In all the Austen novels, the heroine is confronted with living, not Life: and to demand unambiguous experiences is to place oneself at the mercy of ambiguity itself. It is Marianne's belief in the purity of her own and Willoughby's motives that finally endangers and almost destroys her.

This respect for the actualities of living is the uniting principle of the two strains of Jane Austen's fiction. It is the basis of her rejection of gothic fiction in her first novel, and the animus behind her submerged criticism of Anne Elliot in her last: "The sweets of autumn were for a while put by—unless some tender sonnet, fraught with the apt analogy of the declining year, with declining happiness, and the images of youth and hope, and spring, all gone together, blessed her memory . . . [And] after another half mile of gradual ascent through large enclosures, where the ploughs at work, and the fresh-made path bespoke the farmer, counteracting the sweets of poetical despondence, and meaning to have spring again, they gained the summit of the most considerable hill." (*Per,* p. 85). Anne's "tender sonnet" shields her from the requirements of spring; unlike the farmer, she declines to *make* spring come.

Jane Austen was not an intellectual in the sense in which George Eliot was an intellectual. At the close of *Middlemarch,* the two works that are published, *The Cultivation of Green Crops* and *Plutarch's Lives of Great Men for Children,* are meant ironically to point out the failure of higher purpose within the story, Lydgate's failure to complete the treatise on the primitive tissue, and Casaubon (and Dorothea's) inability to produce *The Key to All Mythologies.* In Jane Austen, partly because she did not write of extremely gifted persons, worldly insignificance and intellectual ordinariness are not important; the real challenge lies in everyday life, and Dorothea's second marriage, like Lydgate's stoic loyalty to Rosamond, would have been seen by Jane Austen with more respect and far less irony than George Eliot bestows.

Like her view of the worldly "contribution," Jane Austen's view of literature is unusual for a writer, and yet consistent with her unflinching fidelity to the available world. People who use books, or the unrealities books may have taught them, as a substitute for life are either naive or despondent. What concerns Jane Austen finally *is* survival in the actual world, and survival involves struggle and sacrifice, varying degrees of sacrifice of both the mind and the heart. Yet survival also calls for cooperation, and through cooperation the struggling existence of the individual is embraced by the general creative striving of the species. "Instead of falling sacrifice to an irresistible passion," Marianne found herself at nineteen "a wife, the mistress of a family, and the patroness of a village" (*SS*, pp. 378-379). Marianne's situation may be a prison, yet it is also a shelter, and one that includes a man and children and the people of a village. It is a mark of Jane Austen's genius that, given her intuition of life, she chose to write about marriage and never gave up writing about it. For the experience of marriage contains within it the very antithetical strains I have been discussing. It involves at once the sacrifice of certain potentialities of the self and the opening up of possibilities that the self alone can never provide: a rich subject matter for novels that inquire into the nature and purpose of civilized life.

How then are subject, style, and structure brought together in Jane Austen's novels? I will answer this question in chapters to come. For now, one sample is enough — a comparison between the openings of *Pride and Prejudice* and *Mansfield Park*.

It is a truth universally acknowledged, that a single man in possession of a good fortune, must be in want of a wife.

However little known the feelings or views of such a man may be on his first entering a neighborhood, this truth is so well fixed in the minds of the surrounding families, that he is considered as the rightful property of some one or other of their daughters. (*PP*, p. 3)

About thirty years ago, Miss Maria Ward of Huntington, with only seven thousand pounds, had the good luck to captivate Sir Thomas Bertram, of Mansfield Park, in the county of Northampton, and to be thereby raised to the rank of a baronet's lady, with all the comforts and consequences of an handsome house and large income. All Huntington exclaimed on the greatness of the match, and her uncle, the lawyer, himself, allowed her to be at least three thousand pounds short of any equitable claim to it. She had two sisters to be benefited by her elevation; and such of their acquaintance as thought Miss Ward and Miss Frances quite as handsome as Miss Maria, did not scruple to predict their marrying with almost equal advantage. But there certainly are not so many men of large fortune in the world, as there are pretty women to deserve them. (*MP*, p. 3)

The subject of both openings is marriage, conceived of in incongruous, counting-house terms which make the presentation ironic. Yet there the similarity ends, for the first passage is hopeful and the second is dismal. Why? Because one is narrated comically and the other satirically.

The narrator of *Pride and Prejudice* resists the social world through a series of hyperbolic or understated dodges. As a result of such dodges, the comic narrators in Jane Austen always renew our faith in the power of the artistic will to reshape experience, to formulate and refine language, and to restructure the commonplace experiences of life. "However little known the feelings or views of such a man may be," the neighborhood presses on to its conclusion: marriage and procreation. The sacrifice is comic, for the narrator offers us an experience of life that can be seen as play; raised above necessity, the comic narrator ranges over the subject for its own sake, with no end in view. (It is the neighborhood that has the end in view.)

The narrative voice of *Mansfield Park* sinks into the social world it describes and submits to that world's language entirely. It is as if the neighborhood itself is speaking: "But there certainly are not so many men of large fortune in the world, as there are pretty women to deserve them." The voice is full of the pressure of necessity, self-protective, cautious, debased, and directed toward an end. The whole passage, as Michael Wood says, "suggests a community seen from the inside, even from its underside."[41]

In contrast, the language of ironic comedy boldly resists the pressure of telling lies in the service of society by stating the lie in comic hyperbole: "It is a truth universally acknowledged, that a single man in possession of a good fortune, must be in want of a wife." Or by stating the truth in understatement: "Mr. Collins was not a sensible man" (*PP*, p. 70). Compare this to a similar description of Mr. John Dashwood in *Sense and Sensibility*: "He was not an ill-disposed young man, unless to be rather cold-hearted, and rather selfish, is to be ill-disposed" (*SS*, p. 5). The description of Mr. Collins states the truth so simply that, amidst the usual subterfuges and inversions of social language, it is amusing. The description of Mr. John Dashwood is sunk so deeply in the lies of polite society that the sentence structure itself dismally parodies the contradiction it expresses.

How does the action of a novel relate to the language that creates it? Comic plots, as I have shown, have comic language; satiric language accords with the satiric outcome of *Mansfield Park*. Yet there are moments in all the novels when the story separates itself from the teller. The freedom of the comic narrator is always checked, for example, when the heroine finds herself in a situation where language cannot save her. When Catherine is cast out of Northanger Abbey or when Emma looks forward to a future without Mr. Knightley, the comic narrator is chastened by necessity. The "light and bright and sparkling" narration of *Pride and Prejudice* contains an incongruously dark moment when Darcy visits Elizabeth at the end of the novel. Observing her mother's unctuous deference to Bingley in Darcy's presence, and unaware that he has come back to propose, Elizabeth thinks: "At that instant she felt, that years of happiness could not make Jane and herself amends, for moments of such painful confusion" (*PP*, p. 337).

Similarly, the imprisoned narrator of satire must contend with the freer imagination of the heroine, who often succeeds in breaking through the language of her social world. *Sense and Sensibility* contains several conversations about the meaning of words in which both Marianne and Elinor essentially refine the language.

And as the love between Anne and Wentworth is renewed, the withdrawn satiric voice of the narrator of *Persuasion* is gradually modulated. Anne herself literally begins to speak more and more frequently until, in the second-to-last chapter, she defends woman's constancy (and her own) in one of the longest and most moving dialogues in the novel. "I will not allow books to prove any thing," she announces (*Per,* p. 234); and we know that the satiric voice is momentarily vanquished. For after all, *Persuasion* is only a book.

2

The Two Prototypes: *Northanger Abbey* and *Sense and Sensibility*

Like Dickens, Jane Austen had a habit of working on two novels at the same time. The relationship between *Northanger Abbey* and *Sense and Sensibility* is similar to that between *Pickwick Papers* and *Oliver Twist*. As the first two completed narratives of each novelist, they represent antithetical moods and energies, which are later combined in a single dramatization in *Persuasion* and *Great Expectations. Northanger Abbey,* the prototype of Austen's ironic comedy, is generally agreed to be her earliest major novel, although the precise order of composition is uncertain. Because of its similarity to the *Juvenilia* and its intention of burlesque, *Northanger Abbey* provides the likely beginning of a discussion of Austen's first mature intentions.

As Q. D. Leavis has suggested, Austen began by defining herself through what she rejected.[1] The evident purpose of *Northanger Abbey* is to burlesque the popular fiction of her day, to carry its conventions and assumptions to an absurd extravagance. Yet behind this parodic structure lies a serious quest to learn not only what fiction should be but what it should do, a quest that is as much involved with Mrs. Radcliffe's readers as with Jane Austen's.

From its outset *Northanger Abbey* is preoccupied with what its reader expects and what its reader will learn. This preoccupation is a characteristic of all the ironic comedies; it may be the basis of their exuberance. The language of *Northanger Abbey* is always darting outward to the reader. The opening description of Catherine seems to have no life of its own, but gains its effect exclusively by bouncing off the reader's expectations. "No one who had ever seen Catherine Morland" would suppose her a heroine. And the closing chapter indulges the novel-reader's illusions with Shandean vengeance, as it turns resolutions of plot and meaning back on him:

> [Eleanor's] husband was really deserving of her . . . being to a precision the most charming young man in the world. Any further definition of his merits must be unnecessary; the most charming young man in the world is instantly before the imaginations of us all. (*NA,* p. 251)
>
> I leave it to be settled by whomsoever it may concern, whether the tendency of this work be altogether to recommend parental tyranny, or reward filial disobedience. (*NA,* p. 252)

The first quotation brings to mind the Widow Wadman tour de force in *Tristram Shandy,* in which the narrator leaves an entire page blank for the reader to fill in his preconception of feminine perfection. We are indirectly invited to do the same for Eleanor Tilney's husband. Aware of the secret processes that go into the reading of a novel, both Sterne and Austen felt the novelist's helplessness before the competitive egotism of the reader's imagination. And the ironic challenge contained in the novel's last words is an admission by the author that her story will be misinterpreted, taken out of context, and absorbed into the private, partisan imaginations of her readers.

Of all the ironic comedies, *Northanger Abbey* is the most intrusive in tone, the most aggressive in intention. The spirit of burlesque is restless and unlimited, bordering on epistemological absurdities. "A family of ten children will always be called a fine family, where there are heads and arms and legs enough for the number" (*NA,* p. 13). Beneath these linguistic extremes, the burlesque plot ranges to and fro; it begins by overthrowing the convention of the heroine and ends by reaffirming it, begins by dismissing horrors and ends by admitting them. The only unifying principle of the variegated burlesque, and its consistent target, is the image of the "reader."

This image expands so readily that almost anyone reading the novel, from Austen's day to the present, is likely to have some delusion unstrung in the reading. The English reader of gothic fiction in the 1790s may represent any naive or complacent reader of extravagant fictions in any civilized society. Austen's burlesque places this reader both inside and outside the story. Readers of *Northanger Abbey* in any age, she knew, were likely to resemble either Catherine Morland or Henry Tilney, to be limited either by gullibility or complacency. For if Catherine must learn that the fantasy of art is not true to factual life, Tilney must learn that it *is* true to actual life, that the moral and emotional intensity of art, even bad art, is actually if not factually real. The adhesive style of *Northanger Abbey* comes from this forced identification between the reader of *Northanger Abbey* and the readers of fiction within the novel.

"No one who had ever seen Catherine Morland in her infancy, would have supposed her born to be an heroine." The "no one" is of course the naive reader who, on opening the novel, expects to encounter a more extravagant world than his own. This naive reader is a consistent target throughout the novel; it is against his exaggerated fancy, as well as the heroine's, that the true proportions of "life" or reality are initially defined. From beginning to end, the reader of *Northanger Abbey* is continually made aware of his tendency to strive beyond the limitations of the story, to make characters more or less than they really are. Consider the scene of Catherine's ignoble return to Northanger. This scene is one of the few events in the novel capable of calling forth our pity; as Edmund Wilson said, isolation from others is always a danger signal in Jane Austen. And yet at just this moment, the narrative voice of *Northanger Abbey* intrudes to decompress our sympathy:

A heroine returning, at the close of her career, to her native village in all the triumph of recovered reputation, and all the dignity of a countess, with a long train of noble relations in their several phaetons, and three waiting-maids in a travelling chaise-and-four, behind her, is an event on which the pen of the contriver may well delight to dwell; it gives credit to every conclusion, and the author must share in the glory she so liberally bestows. — But my affair is widely different; I bring back my heroine to her home in solitude and disgrace; and no sweet elation of spirits can lead me into minuteness. A heroine in a hack postchaise, is such a blow upon sentiment, as no attempt at grandeur or pathos can withstand. Swiftly therefore shall her post-boy drive through the villiage, amid the gaze of Sunday groups, and speedy shall be her descent from it. (*NA*, p. 232)

In a way characteristic of Austen's humor, an emotional event is expressed in material terms as a way of pointing up the vacuity of a popular attitude. Yet the purpose of the irony here is corrective, not malicious. Contrary to what Marvin Mudrick has said, Jane Austen's comic irony is not irrelevant to sympathy; irony in *Northanger Abbey*, in the deepest sense, *is* sympathy. The chief function of the irony directed at Catherine Morland is to force us to see her as she is, ordinary, awkward, and ignorant, rather than as we would like to see her. "She had a thin awkward figure, a sallow skin without colour, dark lank hair, and strong features; — so much for her person; — and not less unpropitious for heroism seemed her mind" (*NA*, p. 13). In all the ironic comedies Austen means to show how sentiment can be hostile to humanity and irony friendly to it. Perhaps this is what George Saintsbury meant by Austen's "not inhuman and unamiable cruelty." For with all her "plainness and profligacy," Catherine is human and amiable, possessing "neither a bad heart nor a bad temper" (*NA*, p. 14). Austen's criticism of gothic and sentimental fantasy is not that it overvalues life but that it undervalues it; it disguises and derogates the truth of what is.

For the complacent reader, however, extravagant fictions may serve another purpose in externalizing and distancing the horrors from within. Like the ruined abbey contrasted to the Georgian mansion, the horror literature of the late eighteenth century represented to its readers the polar opposite of the rationality, grace, and precision of the Augustan age. It is Henry Tilney's national pride, not his family pride, that is offended by Catherine's suspicions: "Remember the country and age in which we live." he indignantly urges her. "Remember that we are English" (*NA*, p. 197). Notions of barbarism and savagery, as Claude Levi-Strauss suggests, are the abstract projections of civilized societies, evidence of unwillingness to admit the barbaric and savage within.

("Every savage can dance" (*PP*, p. 25) is Darcy's contemptuous excuse for not dancing at the ball.) This unwillingness is part of the theme of *Northanger Abbey,* for Jane Austen was aware that the titillation of the audience of gothic fiction (which she assumes to be her audience) depended not so much on the quality of the horrors as on the contrast between the secure world of the reader and the perilous world of fiction.[2] Catherine's belief in a violent and uncertain life lurking beneath the surface of English society is nearer the truth than the complacent reader's conviction that life in England is always sane and orderly. "Catherine, at any rate, heard enough [of the General's motives in evicting her] to feel, that in suspecting General Tilney of either murdering or shutting up his wife, she had scarcely sinned against his character, or magnified his cruelty" (*NA,* p. 247).

Catherine Morland is the first of a series of receptive "readers" in Jane Austen which includes such diverse personalities as Marianne Dashwood, Mary Bennet, Henry Crawford, Captain Benwick, and Anne Elliot. Few authors have registered better the effect of literature on the ordinary reader, or the purposes it may serve for the person who is neither an intellectual nor a scholar. The impact of popular fiction on the young people of Jane Austen's day was as profound as the impact of film in the first half of this century; the mind's impressionability to national myths is proven in both. In *Northanger Abbey,* as I have suggested, the myth has to do with the sanity of English life as contrasted to the depravity of the Continent. When Catherine comes to her first awakening and decides that there is a general "mixture of good and bad" in people, that there are no pure villains, Austen qualifies her realization with a statement that suggests that the real delusion is still intact: "Among the Alps and the Pyrenees, perhaps, there were no mixed characters . . . But in England it was not so" (*NA,* p. 200). Soon after, General Tilney returns to Northanger, enraged by his new knowledge of her relative poverty, and evicts her.

Like Don Quixote, Catherine Morland is overcome by a genre; yet also like Don Quixote, she becomes something beyond herself. The final irony of her story is that the literary myth that has victimized her also creates her. In the opening line of the novel — "No one who had ever seen Catherine Morland in her infancy, would have supposed her born to be an heroine" — the "no one" is not only the reader of gothic and sentimental fiction. It is Catherine herself, who until she reads fiction never thinks to cast herself in the role of heroine of her own life. The new genre of the novel had brought about a new self-consciousness in women; and both *Northanger Abbey* and *Sense and Sensibility* explore and add to the question of feminine self-definition by focusing on women whose reading has altered their sense of self.

What seems to have disturbed Jane Austen most about the fiction written before her own were the dangers inherent in its view of the self, if that view was adopted and acted out by women in real life. A central concept in this view is "sensibility." In both sentimental and gothic fiction, the heroine's quality of being is proved by the depth of her response to life, and so the structure of the fiction is designed to test and illuminate her sensibility. As a result, her capacity to suffer is a badge of her superiority. There was nothing new in this definition of heroism; from Greek tragedy onward, suffering had been the heroic destiny. But when this heroic ideal was embodied in stories of ordinary, contemporary people, the effect on the reader's mind was far from the transcendence of terror that Aristotle had identified. Goethe's story of romantic agony and suicide, *The Sorrows of Werther,* had prompted a rash of suicides throughout Europe after its publication in 1774.

Whereas in tragic literature the hero is identified by his mastery of suffering and death, in sentimental fiction like *Clarissa* the experience of suffering or terror itself marks the quality of being. On her way to Northanger, Catherine is "craving to be frightened"; this is what being a heroine is about. She is disappointed that the abbey is not gothically suited to her need for terror. Jane Austen's first two novels are deeply concerned with the romantic reverence for suffering, and with the dangers this attitude poses for the fragile self. In *Sense and Sensibility,* this romantic attitude is dissected with cold compassion for its victim, Marianne Dashwood, whose refusal to contain her despair almost leads to her death; and in *Northanger Abbey* Austen treats her reader's preference for misery with grim irony when, on the first page, she apologizes that Mrs. Morland did not die in childbirth.

It is in the context of such ironic apologies that the critical concern over the depth of Jane Austen's subject matter becomes so revealing of the modern conception of reality. To modern taste, for example, Eleanor Tilney is a far more suitable heroine than Catherine Morland. Indeed, she is precisely the heroine whom Catherine fails to be on the first page of the novel. Her mother is dead and her father is tyrannical. She is effectively "locked up" at Northanger Abbey. She is graceful and attractive, with a mind that, unlike Catherine's, is propitious for heroism. What is more, she is in love with a man who is not permitted to address her. Elegant, sensitive, and withdrawn, she is made interesting to us by her "habitual suffering." Yet in selecting Catherine as heroine, Jane Austen casts into doubt the value of our more romantic and drastic preferences. Catherine herself learns that she does not have to find out horrors, they find her out soon enough. Yet Austen does not turn the tables with a vengeance, as in the case of Marianne Dashwood. The uniqueness of the story is that Catherine escapes any lasting pain; how much she has learned from her experience is not of interest. As in all the ironic comedies, Austen holds true to the value of escaping suffering to the end.

In *Northanger Abbey* the exuberant parody of convention usually takes the form of a comic assault on the reader. In *Sense and Sensibility* the language has no such target but is a deadly mimesis of convention itself. The narrative of Austen's satire is imprisoned so deeply in the idols of the marketplace that it almost seems to turn inward and feed on itself, as in a novel by Flaubert. The reader then searches for some source of vitality within the novel that has not, paradoxically, been contaminated by the novel's ethos. This source is found first in the sexual vitality of Marianne and Willoughby and more gradually in the searching intelligence of both Marianne and Elinor. In *Sense and Sensibility*, as in the other satiric novels, the imaginative freedom of the heroine is threatened by the deceptions, inversions, and subterfuges that polite language enshrines.

In both her comedies and her satires, of course, Austen is responding to the same problem in the nature of language. In an increasingly democratic society, the conventions of language and behavior are in danger of becoming dislodged from their traditionally understood meanings. We recall Henry Tilney's attack on the word "nice": "Oh! It is a very nice word indeed!—it does for everything. Originally perhaps it was applied only to express neatness, propriety, delicacy, or refinement;—people were nice in their dress, in their sentiments, in their choice. But now every commendation on every subject is comprised in that word" (*NA*, p. 108). It is characteristic of the ironic comedies that the real target here is Henry himself, who is being "nice" to the point of fussiness. Yet he is also articulating a real social problem. In the democratized societies of *Northanger Abbey* and *Sense and Sensibility* it is often impossible to tell who is sincere and who is not. When Eleanor Tilney and Catherine Morland meet for the first time, they greet one another "with simplicity and truth," yet the narrator remarks that not an observation or expression was used by either "which had not been made and used some thousands of times before, under that roof, in every Bath season" (*NA*, p. 72). In the comic world of *Northanger Abbey*, such confusion is not ultimately threatening; Eleanor sees Catherine's virtue through her candor. But in *Sense and Sensibility*, Marianne's inability to detect Willoughby's insincerity almost results in her death.

Jane Austen's novels are full of social climbers who, like Isabelle Thorpe and Lucy Steele, have adopted the language of gentility, with its terms of virtue, courtesy, and sentiment, without adopting the corresponding behavior. In the works of satiric realism, they are highly dangerous forces, usually because they succeed in driving the sensitive members of the educated class, like Marianne and Anne Elliot, into their private worlds in an effort to dissociate themselves from the now debased social forms. "Sometimes I have kept my feelings to myself," says Marianne, "because I could find no language to describe them in but what was worn and hackneyed out of all sense and meaning" (*SS*, p. 97). She speaks like a romantic and we sympathize with her. Yet as the story unfolds we are made aware of the social and spiritual devastation that can result from this withdrawal of the self from the world.

Jane Austen saw that if everyone limited language to the expression of private emotions the resulting anarchy of speech would isolate the individual more fiercely, more mercilessly than any oppressive social framework could do. Marianne suffers from neurosis brought on by repression, as Tony Tanner's description of her sickness explains, and his mention of *Civilization and its Discontents* is entirely apt. Yet her suffering is self-willed, as she herself later admits, and comes from the conscious choice to separate herself from others. Her frustration arises from what Foucault called "the absolute exteriority of other people." To Tanner, this sense is entirely justified: "Marianne is indeed sick, sick with the intensity of her own secret passions and fantasies. What is the nature of the society in which this sickness breaks out, at least as Jane Austen depicts it? It is a world completely dominated by forms, for which another word may be screens, which may in turn be lies . . . society is indeed maintained by necessary lies".[3] Two orders of perception coexist in *Sense and Sensibility*; Tanner's statement applies to the first. The first order, which concludes with Marianne's illness, is dominated by Marianne and Willoughby, who view the established forms as external and therefore at odds with private reality. From this attitude issues a judgment of the sanctity of the individual and the contamination of outward forms. Marianne and Willougby are Blakean in their abhorrence of the insincerity of society, and we sympathize with their impatience and even their contempt for the Middletons and Mrs. Jennings. We feel that for the two lovers—to borrow from Sartre—"Hell is other people!"

But this simplicity of view is lost when we learn that Willoughby is insincere and in league with society all along. Nor can the social group any longer be labeled as hypocritical; Mrs. Jennings's heart is in the right place after all, and even Sir John is capable of right feeling. Marianne's belief in the exteriority of "society" is finally the cause of her pain and isolation. In failing to recognize the interiority of society, its place in the individual's identity and needs, she mistakes Willoughby's character and almost gives up her life. Marianne's small degree of fortitude is easily overcome and she gives herself willingly to sickness and even death—and why? Because fortitude is founded on a conviction of the inner connection of individual beings. Marianne's dissociation from the world is pathological because, to Austen, complete dissociation is impossible *except* through death. When in her delirium Marianne begins to struggle against death, she calls for her mother in a subconscious effort to affirm that primal connection. After her recovery, she is finally aware that her own identity occupies a place in the identity of those who love her and that this connection entails a responsibility: "Had I died, —in what peculiar misery should I have left you, my nurse, my friend, my sister!—You, —who had seen all the fretful selfishness of my latter days; who had known all the murmurings of my heart!—How should I have lived in your remembrance!—My mother too! How could you have consoled her!—I cannot express my own abhorrence of myself" (*SS*, p. 346).

The nature of social forms is far more complex than it may seem. Nowhere is this point made more powerfully than in the ball scene when Willoughby uses the social forms in his rejection of Marianne. As Tanner says, "the severest indictment one can make of the social game is that at this point it lends itself entirely to Willoughby's designs—he can use the respected forms to compound a profound emotional falsity at the expense of Marianne."[4] Yet Tanner omits the scene's final touch, which adds considerably to its profundity. Marianne is in agony, and she instantly begs Elinor to entreat Lady Middleton to take her home: "Lady Middleton, though in the middle of a rubber, on being informed that Marianne was unwell, was too polite to object for a moment to her wish of going away, and making over her cards to a friend, they departed as soon as the carriage could be found" (*SS*, p. 178). Here the social form is benevolent although the observance of it is vacant—and that contradiction is the scene's message, for it is precisely because of persons such as Lady Middleton (possessed of a "cold-hearted selfishness") that rules are established. The social form that provides a disguise for Willoughby's cruelty also provides a protection for Marianne in her misery. This is the paradox of civilized life, felt in all the Austen novels: society is a protection as well as a barrier between the self and the world. Just as table manners were originally established to allow people to eat together and later became party to the minutiae of social divisions, the social forms in Jane Austen are perceived as essentially tolerant, designed to give breathing space to the individual existing with others, even though potentially intolerant and capable of being used to isolate and suffocate him.

To view social forms as lies that oppress and damage the individual, then, is to accept the premise of society's exteriority and to exempt the individual from responsibility not only for his own participation in the forms that may damage him but also for his unconscious enjoyment of those which protect him. For although some social forms do require that lies be told in their support, the intelligent, sensitive characters in Jane Austen are actively involved in altering the observance of forms to admit honesty and meaning. Much of the dialogue in *Sense and Sensibility* among Elinor, Edward, and Marianne, for example, involves making discriminations of language and behavior that are at once more honest and more just. To abdicate this responsibility, as Marianne does in choosing to make language a monologue and behavior a monodrama, is to relinquish a part of oneself, and as Marianne learns, to submit oneself to a force that is more tyrannical and more terrifying than a social form could ever be — the annihilating force of the will in isolation. D. H. Lawrence achieves a similar consistency, though with different emphasis, in his treatment of the idea of solitude. The hero of "The Man Who Loves Islands" disdains the compromise of social life to a gradually increasing extent and at last dies of hunger and cold, but in the enjoyment of complete isolation.

In *Sense and Sensibility* language (and by implication conduct) is not only in danger of becoming a function of each person's private, subjective concerns; it is in danger of losing its interpretive function altogether. To Lucy Steele language is a matter of style, an index of gentility; to Marianne it has become almost meaningless. Elinor is aware of the degeneration of this communal bond, and many of her ideas and judgments reveal attempts to resuscitate its integrity. In her campaign to influence Marianne she does not encourage her to lie and thereby abuse social life but, quite the opposite, merely urges her to recognize the existence of social connections by her conduct and to accord others the same right of complex individuality that she accords herself. Marianne challenges Elinor's "doctrine":

> But I thought it was right, Elinor," said Marianne, "to be guided wholly by the opinion of other people. I thought our judgments were given us merely to be subservient to those of our neighbours. This has always been your doctrine, I am sure."
>
> 'No, Marianne, never. My doctrine has never aimed at the subjection of the understanding. All I have ever attempted to influence has been the behaviour. You must not confound my meaning. I am guilty, I confess, of having often wished you to treat our acquaintance in general with greater attention; but when have I advised you to adopt their sentiments or conform to their judgment in serious matters?" (*SS*, pp. 93-94)

Marianne's standards of behavior are more oppressive in their own way than the accepted forms of convention. According to her dicta, people cannot love more than once and older men cannot love at all. There is no better proof than this that the subjective vision of the individual is too narrow for his own good and the good of his neighbor. Even the imperfect social norms of *Sense and Sensibility* provide a wider space for human behavior than Marianne's standards do, however appealing Marianne's superiority of taste and feeling may be. It is Elinor who urges more inclusive, more liberal standards of judgment, which will allow more room for individual preference within the social frame. Elinor possesses analytical intelligence — she is the first to see Edward's goodness of heart — while Marianne's tendency is to judge, and to judge from the surface. And although Elinor is the first to distrust Willoughby, she is also the first to forgive him.

Yet Marianne possesses great appeal, and most of us would agree that the strength of her attraction lies in her passion. The reader feels a spontaneous concern for her, compelled in part by her youth and in part by the author's broader concern over the problem of how to regulate passion without destroying it. It is clear, we must remember, that her love for Willoughby is an extension of her love for herself: "I could not be happy with a man whose taste did not in every point coincide with my own. He must enter into all my feelings; the same books, the same music must charm us both" (*SS*, p. 17). To the true romantic, passionate love is possible only insofar as the other can be regarded as a projection of one's own self, one's higher self. (Such projection becomes more feasible if the other is a blood-relation, an issue I shall take up in my discussion of *Mansfield Park*.) Marianne's narcissistic attraction to Willoughby has all the appeal that Lionel Trilling considers characteristic of self-love: "There is a great power of charm in self-love, although, to be sure, the charm is an ambiguous one. We resent it and resist it, yet we are drawn by it, if only it goes with a little grace or creative power. Nothing is easier to pardon than the mistakes and excesses of self-love: if we are quick to condemn them, we take pleasure in forgiving them. And with good reason, for they are the extravagance of the first of virtues, the most basic and biological of the virtues, that of self-preservation."[5]

Marianne is sixteen when the novel opens, and her age goes far in explaining the nature of her passion. Like Juliet's, Marianne's is an adolescent passion—dazzling in its very ignorance of the complexity that surrounds it, destructive in its determination to annihilate the forms that restrain it, and devoid of the irony of the adult passion in *Persuasion* or, for that matter, in *Antony and Cleopatra*. This is one reason Marianne's responses are given an edge of caricature—not, as Tanner suggests, because Jane Austen was frightened by her creation, but because Marianne's blindness to the social context in which she moves, and to the conventions within herself, is so total as to become humorous at times. All along, for example, Marianne counts on more luxury from marriage than Elinor; her mere "competence" is equivalent to Elinor's "wealth." And she relies on Elinor's observance of social forms to maintain her own comfort and aloofness in unpleasant company: "Marianne was silent; it was impossible for her to say what she did not feel, however trivial the occasion; and upon Elinor, therefore, the whole task of telling lies when politeness required it always fell" (*SS*, p. 122).

I do not agree with Tanner that Marianne is an early Catherine Earnshaw or Maggie Tulliver and that Austen lacked the courage to investigate the fate of passion existing in society. From its opening, *Wuthering Heights* is a potentially tragic world, which we feel must come crashing down. The world of *Sense and Sensibility,* in contrast, is that of everyday, ordinary life. Austen might have agreed with Fowles that "tragedy is all very well on stage, but it can seem sheer perversity in ordinary life."[6] The watery ending of *Mill on the Floss* resorts to a kind of relieving simplicity that Austen had the artistic assurance to resist. Maggie's death does not, as Tanner suggests, testify to the courage of her creator; it may reveal the opposite, that George Eliot was afraid to imagine for Maggie a life without passion. As suggested earlier, in *Sense and Sensibility,* Jane Austen exchanges an old definition of tragedy for a new one: Marianne does not die of unrequited love; perhaps worse, she survives and lowers her expectations. Austen never injured the complexity of her story through unambiguous endings or through taking the central problem out of the hands of the characters and solving it on another level. At the end of *Sense and Sensibility* Marianne's heart is broken, but she is still alive, thinking. There is a horror in this conclusion that we may not wish to contemplate. It is not the conclusion of a writer who lacks courage.

There are no unmixed forces in Jane Austen. Tony Tanner perceives metaphysical contrasts that, to Jane Austen, were not valid: "Elinor wants to know about the social man—man the housebuilder. Marianne is interested in the more primitive, even the more Dionysiac man—man the dancer."[7] Willoughby, as Tanner later admits, is a second-rate dancer indeed, and Colonel Brandon, the housebuilder, is the true lover. Similarly, the abstract notion of society as a force distinct from and outside of the spirit is an illusion derived from Lockean liberalism, created to maintain belief in the individual's innocence and in his separation from an increasingly complex and frightening society. Jane Austen could never see man as anything but the father of the child, adult in the knowledge that while he is a man, he is also a father, and unalterably, a son. To Jane Austen man is not a solitary animal, and as long as social life survives, self-realization cannot be the supreme principle of ethics.

The flashes of self-realization in Jane Austen are always followed by marriage. Anne Elliot is the exception, and her sorrow is a direct result of the failure of her marriage to take place. Even in the space between Marianne's enlightenment and her marriage to Colonel Brandon she confirms her commitment to others: "I shall live now solely for my family. You, my mother, and Margaret, must henceforth be all the world to me" (*SS*, p. 347). The individual achieves spiritual completion through others. This is why no compromise between the opposing forces of the novel, between "passion and reason, impulse and restraint, feeling and form, poetry and prose," is achieved in a single individual.[8] Through connection with others, ideally through marriage, the different aspects are resolved. Marianne and Elinor, both women who raise the spirit, marry good men who lack this capacity; the opposing tendencies are merged in the single spiritual endeavor of marriage. Like so many of Jane Austen's heroines, Marianne has learned that the self flows into the world, that the self is not free. And although her enlightenment is tragic, she does survive. At least it cannot be said of her, as Hume said of Rousseau, "he has only *felt* during the whole course of his life."

3

Necessary Conjunctions:
Pride and Prejudice

Certain moments in literature always surprise us, no matter how
many times we encounter them. One such moment is Cordelia's
response to Lear, "Nothing," in the first act of the tragedy. Another is the opening sentence of *Pride and Prejudice*: "It is a truth
universally acknowledged, that a single man in possession of a
good fortune must be in want of a wife" (*PP*, p. 3). Like Cordelia's
unexpected reply, Austen's claim is surprising because we do not
know how to interpret it. Is Cordelia's answer faint or firm, resigned or defiant? In the atmosphere of Lear's complex vanities,
its stark simplicity makes it ambiguous. Similarly, the opening
claim of *Pride and Prejudice* is either an instance of unalloyed
irony or comic hyperbole. Read ironically, it means a great deal
more than it says; read comically, it means a great deal less. Because its targets are unknown, its assurance is baffling. No matter
how we read it, its finality is its irony (or comedy); it holds its
"truth" and the resistance to its truth in one—the quintessential
stance of the ironic comedies.

Such instances are very few and brief in Jane Austen. They constitute a direct address from the author to the reader. They dazzle
us partly because they are infrequent, and they provide in their
flashing ambiguity a highly concentrated version of the novelist's
perspective. The discourse of the rest of *Pride and Prejudice* issues
from this initial stance and falls into two broad categories, narrative and dialogue. Perceived together, as they are meant to be perceived, the narrative and the dialogue achieve the same brilliant
ambiguity of the authorial voice. Consider the first appearance of
narrative comment in the novel, at the close of chapter 1:

> Mr. Bennet was so odd a mixture of quick parts, sarcastic
> humour, reserve, and caprice, that the experience of three

and twenty years had been insufficient to make his wife understand his character. *Her* mind was less difficult to develop. She was a woman of mean understanding, little information, and uncertain temper. When she was discontented
she fancied herself nervous. The business of her life was to get
her daughters married; its solace was visiting and news. (*PP*,
p. 5)

Considered in isolation, the passage seems objective, informative,
and unambiguous. Yet when read as the conclusion of the following dialogue, the passage achieves a different resonance:

"My dear Mr. Bennet," said his lady to him one day, "have
you heard that Netherfield is let at last?" Mr. Bennet replied
that he had not.
"But it is," returned she; "for Mrs. Long has just been
here, and she told me all about it."
Mr. Bennet made no answer.
"Do not you want to know sho has taken it?" cried his wife
impatiently.
"*You* want to tell me, and I have no objection to hearing
it."
This was invitation enough. (*PP*, p. 3)

Here we have a world of opinion and report, and one in which the
effect of an event takes the place of the event itself. Neither time
nor place is specified except as "day" and "neighborhood." We
have only the disembodied voices of wife and husband clashing in
an empty space, and ricocheting back in the form of countless am-
plifying ironies to the novel's opening statement. The sensibility of
the dialogue is ephemeral, irrational, opinionated; it is a
precarious world indeed to be followed by such stable, definitive
evaluations as "She was a woman of mean understanding" or such
simplistic understatements as "Her mind was less difficult to
develope." This ostensibly objective narrative voice is true as far as
it goes. It is true because its evaluations are, as evaluations,
correct and useful. They are the necessary simplifications we live
by, and the Bennets live by, for the paragraph reveals each as seen
by the other.
Yet these evaluations cannot be mistaken for life itself, and Jane

Austen knows they cannot. When Elizabeth returns from visiting Mr. and Mrs. Collins and her mother asks whether they "do not often talk of having Longbourn when your father is dead," we are surprised. We are required once again to acknowledge the audacity and variety and complexity of this woman's "mean understanding." The cadence of moral rationalism, the abstract, judgmental sensibility revealed in such statements as "mean understanding, little information, and uncertain temper" are always checked by action and dialogue. Through the careful juxtaposition of narrative and dialogue, Austen prevents us from investing everything in such statements.

Elizabeth too must learn that simplifications are dangerous; both she and Darcy insist on what is only provisional and half-true as final. Of her complacent division of humanity into intricate and simple characters, for example, Elizabeth comes to say, "The more I see of the world, the more am I dissatisfied with it; and every day confirms me of the inconsistency of all human characters, and of the little dependence that can be placed on the appearance of either merit or sense" (*PP*, p. 135). The irony of the novel's opening sentence lies in its assurance in simplification and generalization, its insistence that the local perception is universal, absolute, permanent. We simplify our world in order to live in it; and Austen (like Sterne) keeps telling us we do. *Pride and Prejudice* is an exhilarating work because it turns us back continually on life by showing us the failure of language and the individual mind to capture life's unexpectedness. And beneath the exhilaration lies an affection for the bizarre actuality of things. The opening hyperbole, for example, contains an element of eccentric delight in human exaggeration.

The narrative voice, then, provides some limit, some barrier, which the action strives ceaselessly (and successfully) to overcome. The narrator's provision of certitude, despite its accuracy, is temporary. Nevertheless, its role in the novel is of vital importance. Indeed, without the narrative voice, the moral structure of the novel would crumble. The terms of order in the novel are defined by the narrative voice, just as the terms of anarchy are defined by dialogue and action. In this respect, Austen works in a way similar to that of George Eliot. Eliot's compassionate narrative voice is used both to reprimand and to redeem the failing world of Middlemarch. Austen's rational narrative voice is used both to abuse and applaud the evasions of humankind—abuse the cruelties and applaud the abundance. Only through the careful and complex juxtaposition of action and narrative does each author maintain her ambiguity. The depth of both *Pride and Prejudice* and *Middlemarch* depends on the reader's sensitiyity to the relationship between the action of the characters and the voice that enfolds it. As James wrote, we cannot speak of incident and narration as though they were mutually exclusive:

> I cannot . . . conceive in any novel worth discussing, of a passage of description that is not in its intention narrative, a passage of dialogue that is not in its intention descriptive, a touch of truth of any sort that does not partake of the nature of incident, or an incident that derives its interest from any other source than the general and only source of the success of a work of art—that of being illustrative . . . I cannot see what is meant by talking as if there were a part of the novel which is the story and a part which for mystical reasons is not.[1]

In Austen, the "story" is made meaningful by narrative intrusion; and "description" or reflection is made meaningful by story.

Jane Austen's narrative voice establishes a stability in a world of fluctuating opinions and exaggerations. The opening page of chapter 2, for example, dwells on the various "reports" of Bingley and of the party he will bring with him. Bingley is "wonderfully handsome" and "extremely agreeable," and he is bringing "twelve ladies and seven gentlemen" to the next assembly with him. In conclusion (and not wholly in defiance) of these reports, the narrator comments: "[The party] consisted of only five altogether; Mr. Bingley, his two sisters, the husband of the eldest, and another young man . . . Mr. Bingley was good looking and gentlemanlike; he had a pleasant countenance, and easy, unaffected manners" (*PP*, p. 10). This pattern is characteristic in Jane Austen: the responses to an event are catalogued, beginning with the most exaggerated and concluding with the true fact of the case, or the truest response.

The Bennet family's response to Mr. Collins's engagement to Charlotte Lucas is another example of this progress toward truth. Sir William Lucas comes to Longbourn bearing the news, and the first reactions are attributed to the least rational of the group: "Mrs. Bennet, with more perseverance than politeness, protested he must be entirely mistaken, and Lydia, always unguarded and often uncivil, boisterously exclaimed, 'Good Lord! Sir William, how can you tell such a story?—Do you not know that Mr. Collins wants to marry Lizzy?' " (*PP,* p. 126). After Sir William's departure, the responses flow with enthusiasm, beginning once again with Mrs. Bennet and Lydia, to Mr. Bennet, Jane, and finally Elizabeth, whose simple statement truly evaluates the event with regard to her friendship with Charlotte. "Elizabeth felt persuaded that no real confidence could ever subsist between them again" (*PP,* p. 128). This pattern, with its suggestion of the endless variations and subterfuge surrounding an event, implies a belief in the difficult accessibility, perhaps the inaccessibility, of truth. The reliable interpretation of a chapter or incident is usually founded on the response or evaluation stated last.

The conclusions to the ironic comedies are especially ambiguous in this respect. Each has its own ironic touch, each calls to mind the memory of some incident of absurdity or insensibility and in so doing, gently undermines the conspicuous gaiety of the marriage union. The allusion to an imperfection is often injected in the penultimate lines of the last chapter (Lady Catherine's visit to Pemberley, Mrs. Elton's opinion of Emma's wedding clothes) just before the perfect happiness of the union is proclaimed. It is as if the modes of resistance to the truth become part of the truth itself.

The paradox of truth and truth's compromise accounts for the paradoxical mood of uncomfortable harmony with which most of the novels close. Emma's "perfect happiness" and Anne Elliot's "perfect felicity" have the slightly unsettling effect of flattery. Emma is still not above making fun of Robert Martin, as she does in a closing dialogue with Mr. Knightley, and Anne Elliot assures herself that she was right to reject Wentworth in the first place. In a world that the novels themselves have so insistently pronounced to be relative, how can we accept the absolute assertions of the endings? Their ambiguity is intended and is a way of pointing out life's compromise of felicity without derogating what felicity remains. By the time we reach the conclusion of *Pride and Prejudice* we understand the limitations of such words as "perfect" and know how to interpret them; when we close the pages of *Emma* we have learned enough about Emma and Mr. Knightley and Highbury and life in general there to know exactly how much perfection and how much happiness are included in the narrator's "perfect happiness."

The narrative voice, then, possesses the essential perspective of the novel. Although Austen's style has been compared to that of Henry James, her use of a vigorous and daunting narrative voice distinguishes them. This voice has more in common with that of the George Eliot narrator, whose all-inclusive compassion envelops the divisions and decay of the story, or that of the Fielding narrator, whose humor is equally tolerant. Austen's authorial consciousness is also binding, for it accepts in its embrace the evasions and irrationalities of direct dialogue and the cool, clear cadence of reason of the objective narrative. It brings them together in its brief flashes of genius, such as in the opening sentence of *Pride and Prejudice*. In such moments, the two streams of discourse in Jane Austen, narration and dialogue, rush together completely. They represent the *effect* of the novel, the total perspective we are to gain, one that rises spontaneously out of the interaction between narration and dialogue.

It may seem to belie Austen's morality to insist that the evasions and even cruelties that arise from the insensibility or partial insight of the characters of *Pride and Prejudice* are somehow sanctioned by the author. Yet the acceptance of such things is securely encompassed in her wisdom, just as Lady Catherine is finally received at Pemberley. And often, particularly in the ironic comedies, the modes of resistance to what is right or true are fairly innocent. The desire to make Bingley more handsome than he really is, to make his party larger than it really is, reveals a need to make ordinary life more glamorous and drastic than it really is. Emma's requirement that life in Highbury be more vivid, elegant, and mysterious than it is reveals a similar need. It is one of the paradoxes of Austen's perspective that such requirements are both ferocious and innocent.

Pride and Prejudice, however, deals less with the problem of accepting an inelegant and unpoetic world than with accepting an irrational and absurd one. If Emma's aspirations are for more witty and more alive surroundings, Elizabeth's efforts are to restrain the anarchic energies of cynicism and insensibility in her parents. The unrelenting invasion of sense by nonsense, of sensibility by moral nullity, of humor by nihilism is a dominant theme in the novel. And determining the proper moral posture to adopt in such a world is the dilemma of individuality.

Space in *Pride and Prejudice,* as Van Ghent suggests, is "a place for an argument." The psychic and moral distances in the novel are enormous, while the physical distances are a matter of a coach ride. The internal distance between Elizabeth and her mother, for example, we intuitively recognize to be a central structural element in the novel. Distances such as these establish the terms of sensibility and anarchy in the action. Yet what are the terms? Mrs. Bennet moves in an atmosphere of repugnance that is scarcely explained. Studies of Austen's language have insisted that the moral scale of the novels is located in speech—yet is this enough? The variations in diction and sentence structure provide clues to the moral scheme, but they should of course be connected to incident.

Mrs. Bennet and two other reprehensible characters, Lydia and Mr. Collins, as independent personalities, are each characterized by a failure to distinguish the important from the trivial, the valid from the invalid. In language and action, they have no true discriminating sense. Their failure is both intellectual and moral; part of the underlying philosophy of *Pride and Prejudice* is a belief in the intimate bond between intelligence and morality, articulated so well in Richard Simpson's term "intelligent love" or James's "emotional intelligence." Consider Mrs. Bennet's behavior upon learning that Lydia will be married, perhaps her most offensive display in the whole novel.

> It was a fortnight since Mrs. Bennet had been downstairs, but on this happy day, she again took her seat at the head of her table, and in spirits oppressively high. No sentiment of shame gave damp to her triumph. The marriage of a daughter, which had been the first object of her wishes, since Jane was sixteen, was now on the point of accomplishment, and her thoughts and her words ran wholly on those attendants of elegant nuptials, fine muslins, new carriages, and servants. She was busily searching through the neighborhood for a proper situation for her daughter, and, without knowing or considering what their income might be, rejected many as deficient in size and importance. (*PP*, p. 310)

When, however, Mr. Bennet reveals to her "amazement and horror" that he will not advance a guinea to buy clothes for his daughter, Mrs. Bennet's astonishment knows no bounds. In a manner characteristic of Austen's narrative technique, the final sentence of the paragraph identifies the moral problem that the paragraph has been examining: "That his anger could be carried to such a point of inconceivable resentment, as to refuse his daughter a privilege, without which her marriage would scarcely seem valid, exceeded all that she could believe possible. She was more alive to the disgrace, which the want of new clothes must reflect on her daughter's nuptials, than to any sense of shame at her eloping and living with Wickham, a fortnight before that took place" (*PP*, pp. 310-311). Unable to distinguish significant from insignificant experience, Mrs. Bennet can never see below the surface and views, for example, Mr. Gardiner's sacrifices on behalf of her daughter as an early Christmas present.

The shamelessness of Mrs. Bennet's response is both an intellectual and a moral failing. Lydia, educated and admired by her mother, is the best example of Austen's understanding of ingratitude. Lydia is not ungrateful in the way of Goneril and Regan; she is without shame, unconscious of the suffering and inconvenience she exacts from others. Lydia's behavior at the Gardiners' house in London at the time of her wedding exemplifies her shamelessness.

While she is dressing for the ceremony, Mrs. Gardiner is trying to impress upon her some consciousness of her actions. Lydia says, "However I did not hear above one word in ten, for I was thinking, you may suppose, of my dear Wickham. I longed to know whether he was wearing his blue coat" (*PP,* p. 319). In another situation the preoccupation with the blue coat would be humorous; here, because it brings to mind Mrs. Gardiner's painful version of the story, it only signifies the waste of suffering and effort behind the event about to take place. Lydia's blindness is a matter of both the mind and the heart. In her letter of elopement to Mrs. Forster— "My Dear Harriet, You will laugh when you know where I am gone" (*PP,* p. 291)—she reveals a numbness of perception as well as of feeling.

An important technique of moral comment, and certainly of comedy, is the suggestion or juxtaposition of antithetical experiences. When Mrs. Bennet equates Jane's face with the fat haunch of venison as two things that must impress Bingley about her table, an almost metaphorical effect results, an effect that Austen's novels are frequently said to lack. Mr. Collins's equations are even more astonishing; when he learns that the eldest Bennet daughter is engaged, he accommodates himself: "Mr. Collins had only to change from Jane to Elizabeth—and it was soon done— done while Mrs. Bennet was stirring the fire" (*PP,* p. 71). As Collins himself admits, the choice of wife is the selection of another player at the quadrille table at Rosings. Yet the humor of this mentality is often qualified by a recognition of its danger. Upon Lydia's elopement Mr. Collins makes an extraordinary comparison: "The death of your daughter would have been a blessing in comparison of this" (*PP,* pp. 296-297). Here Mr. Collins's insensibility is instructive, for it reminds us that the event is not tragic, and it forces us to readopt the perspective we may have lost through sympathizing with Elizabeth.

The many outlandish equations in the speech of Mrs. Bennet, Mr. Collins, and Lydia create a powerful force of irrationality in the novel. Such bizarre juxtapositions have a way of neutralizing the whole experience of life. It is their impoverishing, indiscriminate strength that Darcy resists through his intellectual fastidiousness and temperamental rigidity. He does not know, he says, more than six accomplished women in his acquaintance; and he will not participate in company that he considers inferior. But while his intelligence makes discriminations to excess, his moral sense, as he says, is lost in the realm of "theory." Bingley and Jane are at the opposite pole; to Bingley, all women are accomplished, and Jane (as Elizabeth complains) has liked too many stupid men. Because their moral optimism is untempered by any real intellectual penetration, they are rendered powerless. Bingley can be persuaded that Jane never cared for him, and Jane lacks the wit to guess what has happened. They are the opposite of Darcy; their good will overcomes their intelligence. Wickham and Charlotte form perhaps the most harmful variation on the moral-intellectual scale in that both have totally inactive moral lives yet highly effective perceptual intelligence. Although Charlotte is a far more sympathetic character than Wickham, both are seducers, always a serious sin in Jane Austen, or to be more precise, both engage in a polite form of prostitution. Mr. Collin's angered insensibility to Elizabeth when she rejects him seems amateur when compared to the calm and knowing insensibility of Charlotte's inviting behavior. Even Lydia seems vulnerable compared to the man who in his careless greed decides to let her seduce him.

All the men and women of Elizabeth's generation are actively involved in adopting their permanent, adult posture toward the world. The decisions and choices of the insensitive or unintelligent characters — Charlotte, Mr. Collins, Wickham, Lydia — are revealed in the way they view the selection of spouse: as a relatively uncomplicated decision, a matter of ambition or necessity. To the intelligent and sensitive person, like Elizabeth or Darcy, the choice of adult posture, like the choice of spouse, is most complex. To a person gifted with "emotional intelligence" in Jane Austen's world, the choice of moral stance in a world that is continually fluctuating under the active energies of sense and nonsense is as problematic as the individual's consciousness will allow. In *Pride and Prejudice* we view a variety of responses: Darcy, who is totally rigid in his refusal to give way to the exigencies of absurdity; Mr. Bennet, who capitulates entirely; Lady Catherine, who exemplifies what her nephew is in danger of becoming; and Elizabeth, who is susceptible to her father's chosen stance. Darcy must learn to laugh at himself and to develop a more generous attitude toward the absurdity of others. Elizabeth is the agent of this change, who has learned the value of laughter from her father, but who, under Darcy's influence, will not give in to it entirely.

Mr. Bennet is one of the most interesting characters in Jane Austen, for through him the author exposes the pieties of cynicism. Mr. Bennet goes beyond seeing the absurdity of life; he *wants* life to be absurd. This attitude is his major failing; his inadequacy as a father is directly related to it. There is a kind of sin, the sin of despair, in wanting life to be absurd, a spiritual lassitude, and in the end a means of self-justification. His well-known statement about the purpose of life, at times mistaken for the author's view, is one of the more chilling comments in all of Jane Austen: "For what do we live, but to make sport of our neighbours, and laugh at them in our turn?" (*PP,* p. 364). This statement recalls Lydia's view that life is a joke. Of her elopement she writes: "What a good joke it will be! I can hardly write for laughing" (*PP,* p. 291).

On the other hand, a numbness to the absurdities of self and others is also associated with moral deficiency. If Mr. Bennet represents the pieties of cynicism, Mary Bennet represents the pieties of sense and signals us to be cautious in assuming an unequivocal Johnsonian value system in the novel. Mary's inflated utterances parody Dr. Johnson:

> Pride . . . is a very common failing I believe. By all that I have ever read, I am convinced that it is very common indeed, that human nature is particularly prone to it, and that there are very few of us who do not cherish a feeling of self-complacency on the score of some quality or other, real or imaginary. Vanity and pride are different things, though the words are often used synonimously. A person may be proud without being vain. Pride relates more to our opinion of ourselves, vanity to what we would have others think of us. (*PP,* p. 20)

Strictly speaking, her words are true, yet she is patently absurd. Like those of Darcy, Mary Bennet's good principles exist in the realm of theory only; when it comes to active goodness, to helping her family during the crisis, she is as selfish as Kitty or Lydia. Austen's belief that sense must be tempered by an appreciation of absurdity is a lasting one. It becomes an issue in *Emma,* particularly with regard to Mr. Knightley, whose only failing is his blindness to the power and pleasure of absurdity. If, like Darcy, we separate ourselves from the anarchic elements of life, we must separate ourselves from the pleasures of expression altogether. It is as though every Elizabeth comes with a Mrs. Bennet, and you cannot have one without the other: in the words of T. S. Eliot, they are a "necessary conjunction." Darcy resists his attraction to Elizabeth in the beginning in part because he cannot tolerate her mother's anarchic vulgarity. Their marriage represents his capitulation to the force of irrationality as it does her surrender to the need for rationality. Similarly, when Darcy will not dance because, as he says, "every savage can dance," he is denying the right of the chaos in himself and others to find form in civilized life; and this is a serious denial in Jane Austen, because only through civilized forms does the chaos of human nature find meaning, and only through the inclusion of chaotic energies does civilization find meaning. Those characters who disavow the importance of emotional and sexual urges in social existence lead surface lives, without resonance and without hope. The world of Rosings is one of meaningless formality, of material luxury and spiritual vacancy, even of ill health. And Charlotte Lucas's life with Mr. Collins is not only a "preservative from want" but a preservative from intelligence, gaiety, and love, an embalmed safety from possibility and the requirement of morality and hope.

The moral activity I have identified — the arbitration of the energies of absurdity by the discriminations of sense and the modification of the egotism of sense by the exigencies of absurdity — is directly connected to the eugenic concerns of the plot. In selecting one another, Elizabeth and Darcy counteract the influences of their parents (in Darcy's case, his surrogate parent) and set forth on an improved project for the present, which is to say, the future. Like the perception of space, the perception of time in *Pride and*

Prejudice is defined internally. Literal time is a few months, just long enough for the marriageable persons to court and marry. Internal time covers the psychic distance of three generations through exposing the actions of the central generation. The past and future do not exist as mysterious abysses; Austen's time is an eternal present, which encloses in its immediate alterations both the past and future.[2] The individual is determined by his past, yet the very existence of this influence ensures the power of his will to affect the next generation. For this reason the choice of mate is the crucial act of life in *Pride and Prejudice,* the one most capable of effecting change and justifying hope.

Pride and Prejudice is far more preoccupied than Austen's other novels with the rituals and taboos concerning mating. In the course of the novel four marriages are decided: those of Charlotte Lucas, Lydia, Jane and Elizabeth; five, if we include Colonel and Mrs. Forster. Every social event is important in affecting the attachments that will result and in forwarding the heroine's education in proper selection. There is neither cynicism nor triviality in thinking these events important; selecting a mate was the arena in which women's whole future was decided. The heroine is the last to be engaged, for part of her knowledge in selection comes through observing her friend and her sisters choose.

As suggested in my discussion of the opening scene, *Pride and Prejudice* is from the beginning a world of unexplained attitudes and restrictions. Characters are judged according to their behavior with regard to these taboos, and the taboos are clarified by the acts that break them. Wickham breaks a powerful taboo in trying to seduce Georgiana and in finally eloping with Lydia; and we know that very careful restrictions surround courtship behavior, such as a limit on the number of times an unengaged couple can dance together at a ball. As Freud specifies, taboos are distinct from moral and religious prohibitions in that they are not based upon any divine ordinance, but may be said to impose themselves on their own account. Almost all the restrictions in Jane Austen's novels appear to the modern reader as taboos rather than moral edicts, because they are unexplained and our own age is no longer familiar with the moral rationale behind them. Like the taboos

Freud describes, the moral edicts in Jane Austen's novels seem to have no ground and to be of unknown origin. Jane Austen does not give explicit reasons for their necessity: those who are dominated by them take them as a matter of course. A modern critic, for example, who sees Lydia's behavior as a positive rebellion of the will reveals that the taboos of seduction and elopement are unintelligible to him. Yet a careful reading of the novel makes these taboos meaningful.

The object of the taboos in *Pride and Prejudice* (like the object of many primitive taboos) is to protect the acts of marriage and sexual function from interference. The marriages of one generation provide the moral ethos for the next; for this reason, it is of absolute importance that marriages be responsible and secure in both the moral and the material spheres. Marriage confers a new moral status on both sexes. A married couple, for example, is allowed to take responsibility for younger, unmarried persons. Shortly after the Forsters are married, they invite Lydia to Brighton; even though Mrs. Forster is as irresponsible as Lydia herself, her new status allows her this authority. Irresponsible and responsible marriages form the basis of the novel's action. Like George Eliot, Jane Austen believed in the power of moral influence. As in primitive custom, those who break a taboo must be shunned, for their example is contaminating; Kitty cannot visit Lydia, Maria Bertram is exiled to a foreign country. On the other hand, the main hope for raising the moral intelligence of the society lies in this belief in the malleability of individual beings.

Marriage of course spawns other chief acts of life: birth, initiation, and, once again, mating and marriage. The first responsibility of parents is to educate and prepare their offspring for participation in this most central process so that they will harm neither themselves or others. Mr. and Mrs. Bennet are guilty of not preparing Lydia for mature initiation into this rite. As a result, her marriage is emotionally vacant and economically irresponsible; the narrative review of the three marriages at the close of the novel informs us that the Wickhams are freeloaders. In a sense, one must raise one's children well so that they will raise their children well. In Jane Austen, one generation is an eternity. What we do now is affected by what our parents did and will affect what our children do. This is the sum of what Elizabeth learns in her passage into adulthood. Only when she understands the extent of her own conditioning is she capable of transcending it: "[Elizabeth] had never felt so strongly as now, the disadvantages which must attend the children of so unsuitable a marriage" (*PP,* p. 236). Her self-knowledge is solidly linked to a knowledge of her past and her family; not until she sees the past borne out in Lydia's fate does she become fully conscious of herself and capable of love.

4

The Victorian Anxieties
of *Mansfield Park*

Virginia Woolf speculated that if Jane Austen had lived to write more novels "she would have stood farther away from her characters, and seen them more as a group, less as individuals. Her satire, while it played less incessantly, would have been more stringent and severe."[1] It would be difficult to find a more legible description of the changes that took place in Austen's style and satire after *Pride and Prejudice.* In *Mansfield Park* Austen achieved a new kind of realism. She did not return to it again until the end of her career, and not even *Persuasion* can equal the exhausting intelligence and overpowering, unanswerable skepticism of *Mansfield Park.* While *Persuasion* may be a more perfect novel, *Mansfield Park* is more ambitious. It does not delight; its vehemence moves us to silence. Those who are familiar with the novels often judge it to be the most interesting, the most intractable to the different schemes of the author's work.

Of all Austen's novels, *Mansfield Park*'s grasp on the memory is the strongest and the most difficult to explain. Edmund Wilson, after thirty years' distance from the novel, recalled the "purely aesthetic sensations" it gave him: "a delight in the focusing of the complex group through the ingenuous eyes of Fanny, the balance and harmony of the handling of the contrasting timbres of the characters, which are now heard in combination, now set off against one another."[2] Again, the sense of "group," of "combinations" is noted. *Pride and Prejudice* is a novel about individuals and is permeated with a sense of their autonomy. The psychology of character in *Mansfield Park* reverses this independence; the individual, powerless to change, is steeped in the ethos of place and circumstance. In *Pride and Prejudice* the individual is too large for the institutions that affect him; in *Mansfield Park,* he is caught immovable in their grip. London, Portsmouth, and Mansfield, the three irreconcilable worlds of the novel, finally come to be seen as Hell, Purgatory, and Heaven, each a place or a prison for the human spirit; and the individual is a citizen with no choice but to yield to the larger motive of his kingdom. If he is called to pass to another, as Fanny is from Portsmouth to Mansfield, he must be ordained into its ways; and those who refuse to be initiated, such as the Crawfords, are inexorably excluded. As Avrom Fleishman has said, the wages of sin is exclusion from Mansfield Park.[3]

The ethos of place and, by extension, of class, is the dominant element in the novel's structure and the essence of its unique realism. Mary Lascelles was the first to note the change in Austen's narrative mode: "In *Mansfield Park* Jane Austen's style develops a new faculty, out of one perceptible in all her novels—a faculty I can only describe as chameleon-like. . . [The] habits of expression of the characters impress themselves on the narrative style of the episodes in which they are involved, and on the description of their situations."[4] The very arrival of the Bertrams' party in the midst of the heavy grandeur of Sotherton, she explains, seems to fasten weights on the style: "Mr. Rushworth was at the door to receive his fair lady, and the whole party were welcomed by him with due attention . . . After the business of arriving was over, it was first necessary to eat, and the doors were thrown open to admit them through one or two intermediate rooms into the appointed dining-parlour, where a collation was prepared with abundance and elegance" (*MP*, p. 84). Mood, action, attitude, and response, or all the elements that make up an "experience" such as the visit to Sotherton, are irretrievably blended, and the effect is a dense, opaque realism—the opposite, for example, of the translucent realism of Tolstoy. Here the event itself weighs on us; no air, no distance separates the reader from the experience. *Mansfield Park* is without a "narrator" as we have understood the term—in the narrator's place is a collective consciousness, the combination of all the intelligences that collect around an event, an "ethos" that is the effect of the event on the group. The result is an uncanny sensation of closeness yet distance, as in a nightmare; the realism of *Mansfield Park* has something of the suffocating yet alluring capacity of the first book of *Paradise Lost*. In the scene of the tour through Sotherton mansion, the sense of close proximity to the event is achieved through a picture of the close group of listeners: "The young people, meeting with an outward door, temptingly open on a flight of steps which lead immediately to turf and shrubs, and all the sweets of pleasure-grounds, as by one impulse, one wish for air and liberty, all walked out" (*MP*, p. 90). *Mansfield Park* is an oppressive novel because of its narration; as in *Bleak House*, the atmosphere of the novel is more powerful than any of its structured meanings—indeed, the atmosphere *is* the meaning. And as in the Dickens novel, the opening page of *Mansfield Park* carries in large part the burden of establishing this mood:[5]

> About thirty years ago, Miss Maria Ward of Huntington, with only seven thousand pounds, had the good luck to captivate Sir Thomas Bertram, of Mansfield Park in the county of Northampton, and to be thereby raised to the rank of a baronet's lady, with all the comforts and consequences of an handsome house and large income. All Huntington exclaimed on the greatness of the match, and her uncle, the lawyer, himself, allowed her to be at least three thousand pounds short of any equitable claim to it. She had two sisters to be benefited by her elevation; and such of their acquaintance as thought Miss Ward and Miss Frances quite as handsome as Miss Maria, did not scruple to predict their marrying with almost equal advantage. But there certainly are not so many men of large fortune in the world, as there are pretty women to deserve them. (*MP*, p. 3)

The grinding sensibility of the narration is lodged in unregenerate ease; the voice is the worn, experienced voice of a class that has allowed its values to be debased. Here marriage is a matter of "luck," subject to the paltry speculations of a lawyer as to the "claim" of the different parties. And the complex varieties of possibility and fate are all subsumed under the shabby, neighborly observation that "there certainly are not so many men of large fortune in the world, as there are pretty women to deserve them." The man of "good fortune" in search of a wife at the opening of

Pride and Prejudice employs a similar irony but to very different effect and with different details. In *Pride and Prejudice,* a local truth is humorously offered as a universal truth, and the neighborhood that abides by the hyperbole is satirized: "However little known the feelings or views of such a man may be on his first entering a neighborhood, this truth is so well fixed in the minds of the surrounding families, that he is considered as the rightful property of some one or other of their daughters" (*PP,* p. 3). In the opening of *Mansfield Park,* the voice speaking is that of the neighborhood itself, and the irony is the kind of smirking irony the neighborhood enjoys. The details of fortune and physical appearance seem like neighborhood gossip. And the notion of marriage in this Northampton community is that of a "match," the literal matching of two commodities: fortune and beauty.

No other Austen novel opens in a mood of such infected emptiness. The brutality evinced in the self-concept of the class as well as in its dealings on the individual plane is but a prelude to the crushing skepticism that follows. *Pride and Prejudice* opens with the miscomprehensions and defects of a neighborhood and a married couple; *Mansfield Park* opens with nothing less than the spiritual condition of the gentry at the close of the eighteenth century.

And this condition is, as Austen sees it, unregenerate. If I were to choose a single term to describe the novel, it would be this quasi-religious word. *Mansfield Park* envisions a world that struggles to renew itself, fails and fails, and finally succeeds minimally. It is a world that is in decline from the outset. The Mansfield estate itself is financially dependent on the colonial holdings in Antigua and no longer able to support itself. And the class described has failed to educate its young to receive their moral and material inheritance; the eldest son is a selfish and idle spendthrift, content to cheat his brother out of a future income; the daughters are indulged, careless, egotistical. The arrival of the poor relation, Fanny Price, and the suffering that she endures remain the only hope, among many false hopes, for a spiritual regeneration of this world.

Austen's change from a perception of the individual in *Pride* and *Prejudice* to groups or "combinations" in *Mansfield Park* reflects her adoption of the problems and anxieties of a new era. *Mansfield Park* is a work of the early nineteenth century, and it is imbued with that era's unique conception of itself as an age of transition. The novel was published seventeen years before John Stuart Mill made his famous claim, "we are living in *an age of transition* . . . mankind have outgrown old institutions and old doctrines, and have not yet acquired new ones." Mill noted that this had been recognized by the more discerning only "a few years back" and that now "it forces itself upon the more unobservant." But more revealing than these observations is the interpretation that "this is not a state of health but convalescence."[6] The unique meaning of the word "transition" to Victorian intellectuals, I believe, was a kind of sickness or near-paralysis. As in Matthew Arnold's famous lines, there was a sense of an impasse in history, a state of decay only barely mediated by a struggle for renewal—a condition of convalescence.[7] The first great novel of the age, *Mansfield Park*, is saturated with this mood. The heavy, immovable quality of its language, and the downward tendency of the narration of many of the chapters (the predominance of Mrs. Norris, for example, in closing paragraphs) convey a sense of spiritual paralysis that struggles but cannot overcome itself. The paralysis is felt most poignantly in Fanny herself, whose suffering makes her conscious, but whose excessive self-consciousness debilitates her. When Sir Thomas departs on his journey to Antigua, the apathy and even the pleasure of his family are stringently catalogued, while Fanny "really grieved because she could not grieve."

The convalescence that was felt to be a cardinal experience of the times was explained by another prophet of the age as the result of extreme self-scrutiny. "The healthy know not of their health, but only the sick," wrote Carlyle in 1831.[8] Like the mood of laboring transition, the era's obsessive self-criticism is fully realized within the novel in Fanny Price, who even finds it necessary to feel guilty about her treatment of Aunt Norris: "Fanny's disposition was such that she could never even think of her Aunt Norris in the meagreness and cheerlessness of her own small house, without reproaching herself for some little want of attention to her when they had been last together" (*MP*, p. 282). Not one incident or suggestion in the whole course of the novel inspires the reader to pity Mrs. Norris. She lives meagerly out of niggardliness, not necessity. That Fanny should feel required to pity her only reveals, in the context of the novel, the degree of her own self-doubt. Similarly, when Tom Bertram is nearing death with a fever: "Without any particular affection for her eldest cousin, her tenderness of heart made her feel that she could not spare him" (*MP*, p. 428). What is the tenderness of heart that makes up for apathy?

Fanny's evangelicalism has been put forth as a possible explanation of this disposition. Yet the religious overtones of *Mansfield Park* (Fanny as "the lowest and the last" is one of many such overtones) are, in the last analysis, ironic. The world of *Mansfield Park*, the social world at the end of the eighteenth century as Jane Austen sees it, is neither religious nor Christian. The novel's view of Mrs. Norris is secular and judgmental; and Edmund's idea of religion is like Arnold's "morality touched by emotion," a religion of "conduct," which asserts nothing of the personality of God. *Mansfield Park,* as I will show, may be viewed as an examination of the fate of morality without religion, the destiny of moral values in a society that no longer "[looks] forward to a juster appointment hereafter." For this reason, to evaluate the characters of Fanny, Edmund, and Sir Thomas in Christian terms is pointless. They judge their fellows mercilessly, and they never forgive; in this they are hypocrites.But Jane Austen does not mean them to be so evaluated. Fanny never claims—nor does the narrative—to feel a Christian pity for Mrs. Norris or Tom, only self-reproach in the case of one and a vague reluctance to "spare" the other. (Fanny, as Edmund says, is a creature of habit.) The standards of the novel are internal; and, as the characters are measured against one another, the terms of measurement emerge as social and psychological.

The causes of the age's self-criticism and the actual truths behind the notion of transition are subjects that have been examined and analyzed by historians and philosophers for well over a century. [9] At the close of the eighteenth century, the gentry were beginning to experience the financial decline that would gather force through the century. The increase in population, particularly in urban population, threatened the traditions of the relatively small gentry. In *Mansfield Park* we witness the gentry's resistance to urban values. The weakening of Christian orthodoxy is suggested during the visit to Sotherton's unused chapel, which only a century before saw the entire household gather regularly for family prayer. The rise of evangelicalism, with its allowance of enthusiasm and tendency to self-scrutiny, is shown in Fanny herself. The gradual breakdown of a social structure of fixed classes is realized in the bare plot of the novel, which includes the rise to prosperity of the poor, lower-middle-class Price children. The challenge to traditional rights and duties of the gentry is felt in several spheres: Maria Bertram is numb to any sense of duty in her role as mistress of an old estate. (Marriage is no longer viewed as a social act, but as a commercial one.) Mr. Rushworth does not feel any more inclined to oversee his estate than does Henry Crawford, who rarely returns to Everingham. The effect of Crawford's absence is hinted when he describes how, on his return, he found several families to be badly off. The economic organization of village agriculture was changing generally because of its inability to remain self-sufficient. Sir Thomas travels to Antigua to secure the colonial holdings that apparently are vital to his financial stability. The historical suggestiveness of the social picture of *Mansfield Park* seems to me to be tolerably profound for a supposedly ahistorical novelist. All of these changes in the economic and social life of the nation are registered in the personal lives of the characters. Yet the personal life is not viewed merely as the passive receiver of exterior influences; the real crisis of the novel has to do with an interior failure — the failure of the individual human spirit to renew itself. Marriage is the highest form of self-fulfillment in Jane Austen, yet the debasement of this most primal hope is revealed in the three marriages described in the opening of the novel. From its economic to its spiritual condition, the world of *Mansfield Park* is a world in transition and decline.

The uncertainty of mind, and hence the self-scrutiny and melancholy, that must arise from rapid changes in so many spheres of life is easily understood. In a time of change, people feel unmoored and are more prey to their own irrationalities. Melancholy, as Robert Burton suggests, is the result of the individual's deep maladjustment to the environment. *Mansfield Park's* melancholic tone may help to explain its popularity among Victorians. In many ways, characters such as Fanny and Edmund, whose dispositions border on melancholy, would have held more meaning and interest for Victorians than Elizabeth Bennet or Emma Woodhouse. Contrary to the accepted view, Fanny and Edmund, not the Crawfords, are the children of the future, the Victorians. Mary Crawford in particular is an eighteenth-century type, with her exuberance, wit, and Johnsonian preference for the city.

Another neurosis, xenophobia — so powerful an impulse in *Mansfield Park* — may also account for its interest to Victorians. The English reaction to the French Revolution, the dread of revolution at home, I believe, is partially responsible for the prevailing mood of suspicion and fear in the novel. Among others, Avrom Fleishman has discussed the significance of the play *Lovers' Vows* — its foreign source, its essentially radical content, and the mysterious effect it produces on the underservants at Mansfield.[10]

A fear of contamination pervades the novel. Fanny takes the impropriety of Henry Crawford's behavior personally, as if any impurity within the walls of Mansfield infects all of its inhabitants. Both Fanny and Edmund are pained by the slightest indecorum in the behavior of Mary Crawford; they discuss her disrespectful allusion to her uncle as though she had attacked Sir Thomas himself. The fear of infection at Mansfield has its source in a nineteenth-century myth that has peculiar force in *Mansfield Park* and that was to gather force throughout the century: the belief in the sanctity of the home. Many Victorians came to see the home as the last and only preserver of moral values that were everywhere being debased. The desperation with which Fanny clings to an ideal conception of Mansfield reveals her conviction that this only remaining integrity cannot risk infection. The origin of this emerging concept of home is explained by Walter Houghton as a reorientation of a masculine attitude. In the eighteenth century the coffee house had often been the center of masculine social life, but in the ninteenth century "men's life is more domestic," Mill wrote, because the wives became more their husbands' equals in education. Walter Houghton writes:

> But none of this goes to the root of the matter, for the greater *amount* of the family life and thought would not in itself have created "that peculiar sense of solemnity" with which, in the eyes of a typical Victorian like Thomas Arnold, "the very *idea* of family life was invested." That idea was the conception of the home as a source of virtues and emotions which were nowhere else to be found, least of all in business and society. And that in turn made it a place radically different from the surrounding world . . . [In] Ruskin's definition in *Sesame and Lilies* . . . [it is perceived as] both a shelter *from* the anxieties of modern life, a place of peace where the longings of the soul might be realized [if not in fact, in imagination], and a shelter *for* those moral and spiritual values which the commercial spirit and the critical spirit were threatening to destroy, and therefore also a sacred place, a temple.[11]

Mansfield Park was written at the end of the long and grim struggle with France, and in times of war the home is idealized both by those taken away from it to fight and those who remain to feel their absence and the fear of invasion. Attachment to the enclosed serenity and regularity of home is strong in *Mansfield Park*; Sir Thomas feels it deeply upon his return from Antigua, and the narrator judges his sons and their friends according to the degree of their own attachment to domestic comforts and quiet.[12] The Mansfield household is invested with the solemnity that Houghton describes. Indeed, one of the remarkable characteristics of the house is the ban on levity that Sir Thomas's presence exercises, a restriction that causes the sullen discontent of his daughters. (Levity is what Queen Victoria found "not amusing.") Often seen as a nostalgic vision of late-eighteenth-century domesticity, Mansfield is in many respects a Victorian household, from its deference to Sir Thomas to its bourgeois disapproval of the idle aristocrat Mr. Yates. And among all the complicated objections to the theatricals, the largest and most powerful is the fear of disruption, the sense that the sanctity of Mansfield will be violated if its rooms are no longer its rooms and its children no longer its children.

The unregenerate spiritual mood felt at the opening of the novel—the resistance of the class described to a higher conception of marriage, and the resistance of the individuals described to a higher conception of the moral life—is vital to an understanding of what follows. For the two major events before the return of Sir Thomas (the visit to Sotherton and the theatricals) are envisioned as virtually metaphysical attempts at regeneration. The desire for improvements at Sotherton reveals a craving for a new order of environment and the impulse to extinguish the old environment. And the play-acting represents a yearning for a new order of personality and a desire for the extinction of the old personality. In both events, what is important is not the implications of an interest in picturesque landscapes or the moral objections to *Lovers' Vows,* but the desire for the events themselves, and the need felt by almost all the characters for an experience that will take them either literally or psychically out of the unregenerate world of Mansfield Park. Nowhere in Jane Austen is the sense of collective desire portrayed more brilliantly than in these events, which hold so much hope and yield so much disappointment. Each experience has the same rhythm: the suggestion, always skillfully pushed forward by Henry Crawford, the instantaneous enthusiasm of the group, the pleasure with which it is initiated, the growing sense of evil, and the flowering of universal discontent.

That the visit to Sotherton is from the outset fraught with expectation and importance to almost everyone is brought out in the endless debate over who will be allowed to attend, how they shall be transported, and even where each person will sit in the conveyance. Yet Sotherton disappoints and is metaphorically conceived as a fallen world, from its vacated chapel to its "wilderness" where the Crawfords begin to exert their sexual temptation—Henry leading Maria away from her fiancé and Mary drawing Edmund away from Fanny. As Fleishman suggests, "the elements of diction and imagery in the scene conspire to convince us that we are not only in the presence of the introduction of evil into the little world of the Mansfield set but also in the presence of an eternal human situation."[13] The imagery Fleishman mentions includes the setting of the action in the "wilderness," the enclosure of the wilderness by iron gates which the illicit lovers try to pierce, and the insidious penetration of the enclosed area by serpentining walks where Fanny and Edmund lose themselves. The diction includes snatches of a dialogue like Julia's refusal to "punish" herself for her sister's "sins" and her feeling that she has been doing "penance" by being paired with Mrs. Rushworth. Finally, on the return home, the event that held so many different expectations leaves its partici- pants in a mood of dejection: "Their spirits were in general ex- hausted — and to determine whether the day had afforded most pleasure or pain, might occupy the meditations of almost all" (*MP,* 106).

The acting scheme is equally spontaneous and equally disap- pointing. After the initial inspiration and the enthusiam of all ex- cept Fanny and Edmund are recorded, the mood of the group be- gins to decline almost immediately; Crawford's complicated pleasures lend an atmosphere of evil, and almost a week of bicker- ing ensues over the choice of play (each person has a specific notion of the personality he wishes to assume). Edmund finally succumbs in a particularly ugly scene in which his brother and sisters try to suppress their smiles. And finally, "every body began to have their vexation" and the mood of the party is almost totally discontented. When the first complete rehearsal is at last to take place, Mrs. Grant is ill and Fanny is urged by all, even by Ed- mund, to take her place for the evening. This infection is com- plete at last when Fanny complies. At this moment, Sir Thomas appears.

Sir Thomas's return is like a rebuke to the corrupted aspirations of his household. Though the novel does not develop his experi- ence in Antigua, it has apparently been a profound one. He is "grown thinner" and has a "worn look of fatigue." His tempera- ment has changed: he is kind to Fanny, and he is deeply moved to be with his family again. For the first time, he looks at his household objectively and recognizes its failings, particularly in the dangerous influence of Mrs. Norris: "His opinion of her had been sinking from the day of his return from Antigua." After explaining the particular situation of the colony at that time, Fleishman advances an interesting theory of what happens to Sir Thomas in Antigua:

> He goes to Antigua as a planter, presumably opposed to abolition; he occupies himself, for economic reasons, with improving the slaves' conditions. He acquires some of the humanitarian or religious message of the Evangelical and other missionaries laboring in the same vineyard; and he returns critical of his own moral realm, with a warmer feeling for his young dependent, a sterner rejection of aristocratic entertainment (especially that with a marked revolutionary content), and a strong defense of his son's dedication to resident pastoral duty.[14]

Whatever actually occurs, it is clear that Sir Thomas has suffered and that his suffering and separation have begun to awaken in him a knowledge of what to value and how to value it. Consistent with the closing theme of the novel, only those with a "consciousness of being born to struggle and endure" inherit the "earthly happiness" that by the close of the novel, is to be found at Mansfield Park.

From Sir Thomas's return to Fanny's trip to Portsmouth, the narrative is preoccupied with another series of efforts to renew the self—this time through love. Even Maria Bertram's marriage is described as an effort to launch herself in another world, that of London. And, like all the attempts to escape Mansfield, Maria's attempt fails; she finds that "Mrs. Rushworth [can be made] Maria Bertram again." But the true hope for renewal is found in two other pairs: Edmund and Mary Crawford, and Fanny and Henry Crawford. As critics have often pointed out, the dialectic of *Pride and Prejudice* (or more emphatically, the dialectic of *Sense and Sensibility*) is realized in these pairs: the classical values of character and reason and the romantic values of personality and emotion are set off against one another. Yet the synthesis is thwarted; and its failure is often identified as the most uncharacteristic thing about *Mansfield Park* in the Austen canon.

Lionel Trilling's essay on *Mansfield Park* has done much to dispel our dissatisfaction with the novel's final renunciation of the Crawfords. Of Mary Crawford he writes persuasively: "[Although] on a first reading of *Mansfield Park* Mary Crawford's speeches are all delightful, they diminish in charm as we read the novel a second time. We begin to hear something disagreeable in their intonation: it is the peculiarly modern bad quality which Jane Austen was the first to represent — insincerity . . . In Mary Crawford we have the first brilliant example of a distinctively modern type, the person who cultivates the *style* of sensitivity, virtue and intelligence."[15] Yet for all the modern vacuity of the Crawfords' assertive personalities they are capable of love and they do love. Their actual and potential love for the sober children of Mansfield is one of the most hopeful aspects of the novel. We instinctively admire the courage of love between opposites. Mary Crawford's love for Edmund is the best part of herself; her only weakness is an unwillingness to acknowledge it: "There was a charm, perhaps, in his sincerity, his steadiness, his integrity, which Miss Crawford might be equal to feel, though not equal to discuss with herself" (*MP*, p. 65). And her profusion of "sweet remembrances" when she returns to the room where she has rehearsed a love scene with Edmund reveals the distance she has traveled in her willingness to consciously appreciate his worth.

"I think I see him now . . . through the two long speeches. 'When two sympathetic hearts meet in the marriage state, matrimony may be called a happy life.' I suppose no time can wear out the impression I have of his looks and voice, as he said those words . . . That very evening brought your most unwelcome uncle. Poor Sir Thomas, who was glad to see you? Yet, Fanny, do not imagine I would now speak disrespectfully of Sir Thomas, though I certainly did hate him for many a week. No, I do him justice now. He is just what the head of such a family should be. Nay, in sober sadness, I believe I now love you all." And having said so, with a degree of ten-

derness and consciousness which Fanny had never seen before
. . . she turned away for a moment to recover herself. (*MP*,
pp. 358-359)

We cannot but feel that Edmund's influence, had they married,
could have modified the unruly skepticism of her mind, which so
appalls him. Her words are filled with a sense of heartfelt surrender.

Henry Crawford's interest in Fanny has its origins in pure egotism, yet develops into a powerfully earnest and loving recognition
of her goodness. We are made to feel that his love, like his sister's
(if only because *he* feels it) contains his "salvation": "You have
some touches of the angel in you, beyond what—not merely beyond what one sees, because one never sees anything like it—but
beyond what one fancies might be. But still I am not frightened. It
is not by equality of merit that you can be won. That is out of the
question. It is he who sees and worships your merit the strongest,
who loves you most devotedly, that has the best right to a return.
There I build my confidence" (*MP*, p. 344). "Would he have per-
severed," we are told, "Fanny must have been his reward." And
his loss of "the woman he had rationally, as well as passionately
loved" becomes the great regret of his life, his self-created hell, as
we learn in the final chapter when the catalogues of the saved and
the damned are enrolled.

As Avrom Fleishman has shown, *Mansfield Park* is filled with
the language of Evangelical eschatology, emphasizing salvation
through faith, without specifying the nature of the object of faith.
London, Portsmouth, and Mansfield are, by the close of the
novel, perceived as the three discrete and irreconcilable kingdoms
of Hell, Purgatory, and Heaven. "Without presuming to look forward to a juster appointment hereafter," the novel applies the
moral and eschatological terms of religion to this life; indeed,
Mansfield Park would have been rich material for a chapter in J.
Hillis Miller's *The Disappearance of God*. Let us consider the
three kingdoms.

From *Northanger Abbey* onward, London is a "town of Vanity," the great danger to morality and stable personal relationships

in Jane Austen.[16] Jane Bennet remains in London for months without encountering Bingley, and it is in London that Willoughby commits his vilest treachery toward Marianne. The image of London is powerful enough to emerge in Marianne's delirious utterings: "Marianne, suddenly awakened by some accidental noise in the house, started hastily up, and with feverish wildness, cried out — 'Is mama coming? — ' 'Not yet,' replied the other, concealing her terror, and assisting Marianne to lie down again . . . 'But she must not go round by London,' cried Marianne, in the same hurried manner, 'I shall never see her, if she goes by London' " (*SS*, p. 311). Even the clergy is powerless to counteract the overwhelming and irrational social world of London. As Edmund says in his defense of the effectiveness of clergymen in the country, "The parish and neighborhood are of a size capable of knowing his private character, and observing his general conduct, which in London can rarely be the case" (*MP*, p. 93). In *Mansfield Park,* the dichotomy between Mansfield and London is symbolized in the differences of opinion and temperament between Edmund and Mary: virtue and intelligence, seriousness and wit, nature and society, reason and imagination, morality and art, ritual and chaos. Yet when personified in individuals the choice becomes more complicated, no longer a simple dualism. *Mansfield Park* is a problematic novel because it applies the terms of religion to the social world, and it is caught between its own mythic and fictional concerns. According to the Christian myth, the choice between Fanny and Mary is a choice between virtue and vice; yet in the social context of fiction the terms are changed significantly to a choice between duty and sex, between family love and erotic love.

Similar ambiguities beset the conceptions of Portsmouth and Mansfield. After the worldly efforts at renewal have failed (Fanny refuses Crawford), Sir Thomas sends Fanny back, as one cast out, to her original home in Portsmouth. Here she learns the value of Mansfield, and, in her absence, Mansfield itself is "purged" of its corrupted inhabitants and visitors: Maria and Julia depart, the Crawfords leave, and Tom, the prodigal son, returns home with a violent fever that reforms and chastens him. To the Price children, Fanny, Susan, and William, Portsmouth is a place of suffering or expiation which prepares them for Mansfield. The Bertram daughters are found to be unworthy of Mansfield; unlike Fanny, they never earn its graces through suffering. When Fanny returns to Mansfield, it has gained the aura of paradise: "The change was from winter to summer. Her eye fell everywhere on lawns and plantations of the freshest green; and the trees, though not fully clothed, were in that delightful state, when farther beauty is known to be at hand, and when, while much is actually given to the sight, more yet remains for the imagination" (*MP,* pp. 446-447). This Eden is the only heaven Austen envisions: "The happiness of the married couple must appear as secure as earthly happiness can be" (*MP,* p. 473).

Yet the social implications of the transfer from Mansfield to Portsmouth are quite different. Fanny's response to her natural home and family is perhaps the most excruciating passage of interior monologue in all of Jane Austen.

> She was at home. But alas! it was not such a home, she had not such a welcome, as — —she checked herself; she was unreasonable. What right had she to be of importance to her family? She could have none, so long lost sight of! William's concerns must be dearest—they always had been—and he had every right. Yet to have so little said or asked about herself—to have scarcely an enquiry made after Mansfield! It did pain her to have Mansfield forgotten; the friends who had done so much—the dear, dear friends! But here, one subject swallowed up all the rest. Perhaps it must be so. The destination of the Thrush must be now pre-eminently interesting. A day or two might shew the difference. *She* only was to blame. Yet she thought it would not have been so at Mansfield. No, in her uncle's house there would have been a consideration of times and seasons, a regulation of subject, a propriety, an attention towards everybody which there was not here. (*MP,* pp. 382-383)

What Fanny learns at Portsmouth is the effect of economic status on personality and character. In the words of Lionel Trilling, "after a certain point quantity of money does indeed change into quality of personality: in an important sense the very rich *are* different."[17] What she learns to value at Mansfield is serenity and genteel manners, or the well-regulated personal life that is made possible with money.

The ambiguity that arises from this juxtaposition of religious and social meanings culminates in the final chapter, where, as Fleishman suggests, the saved and the damned are pronounced and placed. Damnation is expulsion from Mansfield Park and what is perceived as its newly discovered bliss. Maria is exiled from England, dwelling with Mrs. Norris "in another country—remote and private . . . shut up together with little society" where their tempers become their "mutual punishment." Henry Crawford, having deviated from the "way of happiness," has lost the "reward" of Fanny. And as if the loss of the woman he loves were not enough, the voice of justice regrets that the double standard of sexual behavior should make "the penalty . . . less equal than could be wished." Mary Crawford is consigned to London for the rest of her unmarried life, unable to "put Edmund Bertram sufficiently out of her head." And of course all the elect are found at Mansfield. Fanny, returning like Clarissa to her "Father's House" is at last received as "the daughter that [Sir Thomas] wanted." Susan and William Price are also included among the elect in the novel's last words, adopting, as it seems, Sir Thomas as their father who "[rejoiced] in what he had done for them all." And the happiness of the married cousins is "as secure as earthly happiness can be." The death of Dr. Grant happily brings the obedient children back to the "paternal abode." Those who are chastened, those with the stoical consciousness of having to struggle and endure, inherit the earthly paradise.

The social resolution revealed in these different destinies is horrifying. Fanny and Edmund, and the values they represent, fail to redeem the Crawfords, either by example or by the influence of love. "We are bidden contemplate," write Sheila Kaye-Smith and G. B. Stern, "not the triumph of evil, but certainly what is not far removed from it, the failure of goodness."[18] London and Mansfield are still the two alien worlds they were in the beginning, blind to one another, ignorant of one another's values, misreading one another's manners. Edmund's description of his farewell visit to Mary Crawford is the shrewdest delineation of this: "She had met him, he said, with a serious — certainly a serious — even an agitated air"; but in her confused fear of the breach her brother's sin may cause, she chatters nervously of "folly." She has never comprehended the solemnity of Edmund's disposition, and her chatter is enough to convince him that he has "never understood her before" and that she is a "corrupted, vitiated mind" (*MP*, pp. 454-458). He ends by seeing her as a temptress, interpreting her last plea, her blushed face and nervous smile, as seductive play. Sir Thomas himself could not be more willfully and blindly principled.

Sir Thomas's sanctimonious and vindictive treatment of his daughter Maria has amazed many readers; for after acknowledging his own part in the failure of her character, he seems willing to forgo his responsibility to her altogether. "Maria has destroyed her own character" and must pay through permanent estrangement from her family. We are reminded of Mr. Collins's notion of Christian forgiveness. Advising Mr. Bennet on how to treat Lydia and Wickham after their elopement, he writes, "You ought certainly to forgive them, as a Christian, but never to admit them in your sight, or allow their names to be mentioned in your hearing" (*PP*, p. 364). Sir Thomas suffers for a time under the knowledge of his own failures, but "time will do almost everything . . . comfort was to be found greater than he had supposed, in his other children" and, we may add, in his new children.

The rise to favor of the Price children, Susan and William, is seen as one of the true hopes for the future at the close of the novel. Susan and William seem to represent the new breed: strong, fearless, able to endure. Yet they are also thick-skinned and a shade opportunistic. William's competitive disposition is made to appear slightly humorous, as in the card-playing at Mansfield Parsonage. And Susan is only too adaptable to the cushioned ease and wealth of Mansfield, quite willing to give up her natural family altogether. Neither possesses the religious disposition and values of Fanny and Edmund, although both willingly adapt themselves to this world. They possess a secular integrity, which is perhaps another term for solid bourgeois values.[19]

The marriage of Fanny and Edmund is consciously invested with hope: "The happiness of the married cousins must appear as secure as earthly happiness can be." Their marriage is one among many virtual brother-sister combinations in English fiction: Heathcliff and Catherine, David Copperfield and Agnes, Mary Garth and Fred Vincy. As suggested in my discussion of *Sense and Sensibility*, the attraction between "like" personalities has its source in romanticism: the other is loved because of his or her share in the self or his representation as a higher self. "Her mind in so great a degree formed by his care," Fanny loves Edmund as a part of herself. Nietzsche, who preferred his sister to other women, wrote to her, "How strongly I feel in all that you say and do, that we belong to the same stock. You understand more of me than others do, because we come from the same parentage. This fits in well with my 'philosophy.'" We know how this sensibility affected Byron; Wagner suggests a similar sentiment in the love of Siegmund and Sieglinde. In Freudian terms, this kind of love reveals a failure to meet the challenge of mature experience, of adult sexuality. Fanny's abhorrence of Henry Crawford from the beginning is not simply one of principle; it includes a distinct distaste for and fear of his sexuality. And Edmund's relationship with Mary Crawford seems, from the outset, difficult and threatening to him. At one point, her attack on his lack of competitiveness may be read as a direct challenge to his masculinity. He seems only too willing to give up the uncomfortable relationship when their siblings run off together. It seems inevitable, convinced as he is that the visit to her in London will be the "last, last interview of friendship," that he should finally judge her to be a temptress. Has not this been his self-protective attitude all along?

In *Psychology of Women* Helene Deutsch wrote of the "eternal feminine conflict between eroticism and motherliness"; in larger terms this becomes the eternal human conflict between family love and erotic love. *Mansfield Park* is par excellence a novel of the inexorable bonds of family love. At the center of the middle volume Jane Austen makes a direct statement on the subject that is uncharacteristic in its emphatic sincerity: "Children of the same family, the same blood, with the same first associations and habits, have some means of enjoyment in their power, which no subsequent connections can supply; and it must be by a long and unnatural estrangement, by a divorce which no subsequent connection justify, if such precious remains of the earliest attachments are ever entirely outlived" (*MP*, pp. 234-235). At the close of *Mansfield Park* Fanny is as much married in mind to her surrogate father Sir Thomas as she is in fact to her substitute brother Edmund. In many ways the pivotal relationship in the novel is between Fanny and Sir Thomas; his approval and his son's love are the final goals of her spiritual struggle. Anticipating Freud, Austen implies that for the woman, the classic sex partners are father and daughter.[20] Yet the incestuous tendency in fiction is conceived less as an infantile fantasy than as a fear of change or death. For if you marry your father, time and history are arrested. The sense of stasis in *Mansfield Park* and *Emma* is partially explained by the incestuous marriages with which they end. The natural order is violated; the father does not die and the son does not replace him. The father becomes the son, the husband, and time stops. This is the darker side of the theme of cooperation in Jane Austen. In *Mansfield Park*, cooperation is a kind of inertia.

Seen in this light, nothing really changes in *Mansfield Park*. We are at the end where we were at the beginning. Susan and Fanny, the two worthy daughters, have simply replaced Maria and Julia, the two unworthy daughters. Edmund, Tom, Sir Thomas, and Lady Bertram remain as they were, only purged—in the case of Sir Thomas, purged of that vicious "part of himself," Mrs. Norris. The action of the novel merely witnesses a series of casualties. Mansfield is still Mansfield—"as thoroughly perfect in [Fanny's] eyes" as it "had long been." The only consolation perhaps is that the marriage with which the novel ends is better than the marriage with which it began. Yet is it? "And to complete the picture of good, the acquisition of Mansfield living by the death of Dr. Grant, occurred just after they had been married long enough to begin to want an increase of income, and feel their distance from the paternal abode an inconvenience" (*MP*, p. 473). To comprehend the full implication of their move we must go back to Sir Thomas's speech on the evils of multiple incumbency:

His going [to the rectorship of Thornton Lacey], though only eight miles, will be an unwelcome contraction of our family circle; but I should have been deeply mortified, if any son of mine could reconcile himself to doing less . . . a parish has wants and claims which can be known only by a clergyman constantly resident . . . [Edmund] knows that human nature needs more lessons than a weekly sermon can convey, and that if he does not live among his parishioners and prove himself by constant attention their well-wisher and friend, he does very little either for their good or his own. (*MP*, pp. 247-248)

Apparently the needs of human nature take second place to the want of an increase in income. Typical of Jane Austen's endings, this last, barely noticeable irony is consistent with the massive irony of the novel itself. The formula I laid out in chapter 1 is present in *Mansfield Park*: the connection between generations, the burden of the past, the burden of the future. Yet *Mansfield Park* gives it this profound and new ambivalence. What then was Jane Austen's intention? Perhaps to expose the effect of religious values on society after religion had died. Lionel Trilling has suggested, following Hegel, the terrible burden on personality that a secular society imposes. *Mansfield Park*'s great achievement is the modern realism with which it conceives of personality, its exposure of the instinct of the will to annihilate the "other" in pursuit of its identity. The novel has no heroine and no hero; not one path can be singled out with honesty; not one is pursued without devastation to another. Fanny and Edmund finally emerge as monsters, if only because they overpower the Crawfords so completely; by the close of the novel the high-spirited villains seem pitiful and defenseless by comparison. After the tyranny of victory, questions of moral sincerity or insincerity seem trivial.

Once again *Mansfield Park* is a transitional work; it is like a raw version of *Middlemarch*, unshielded by the great, compassionate narrative voice which makes that novel's brutality bearable. In exposing horrors without resolving them, *Mansfield Park* is a deeply pessimistic and enervating work. Its profundity is malicious; it exacerbates and finally exhausts us.

5

Civilization and the Contentment of *Emma*

There is a plaguing discrepancy, familiar to anyone who has written on *Emma,* between reading the novel and writing about it. The novel's first great strength lies in the ability to draw the reader in. We are made happy in the traps that are laid for us; we roll in their nets and sleep. We read, in the words of E. M. Forster, with mouth open and mind closed; and after we have finished the spell is broken.[1] Then we can begin to think about it, when the remembered event and the inferred theme have lost their primary, exigent brilliance. The pleasure of reading *Emma,* the very great pleasure, has little to do with the kinds of linear meaning that may be found in most novels; the pleasure comes from our willing immersion in the everyday concerns and relationships of this world, and from a glow of suggestion in the narrative that tells us: this is enough. The novel's very self-absorption makes it acceptable and wonderful. It is a world that believes in itself entirely, and hypnotized, we too believe.

How is this irresistible self-absorption achieved and sustained? There are many answers to this question. One concerns the structure of the novel. Most novels written during the eighteenth and nineteenth centuries, and even many later ones, are teleologically structured—either overtly, like *Pride and Prejudice* and *Great Expectations,* or ironically, like *Tom Jones* and *Vanity Fair.* To miss the outcome of these stories is to miss the meaning. This causal structure is not realized in a few exceptions, notably *Tristram Shandy* and *Emma,* whose conclusions are not, as it were, judiciously weighted. Although we may wonder, like Mr. Knightley, what will become of Emma, her destiny, either social or moral, has little to do with her actions. She is not punished for her misconduct; she does not earn the perfect happiness that is hers in the end. Nor are we disturbed by the non sequitur; although she is often in error, we never feel she is heading toward any retribution except enlightenment. Emma's fate does not identify her the way, say, Isabel Archer's fate makes her Isabel Archer. Emma is always Emma, an integrated, functioning whole; after all her surprises and self-criticism, we still enjoy her in the same way. When she says near the close of the novel, "Oh! I always deserve the best treatment, because I never put up with any other" (*E*, p. 474), we smile at her once again, or perhaps with her. Lionel Trilling calls this structure "forgiving," yet the idea of forgiveness still assumes a causal plot. That Emma is never properly humbled by fate has little to do with pride forgiven, but is a matter of personal being. Because she is Emma, acting out her extraordinary nature from beginning to end, we are satisfied. Our *not* thinking about matters of forgiveness is what makes our immersion in her concerns so effortless.

Just as the structure of *Emma* is not causal, it is also not hierarchical. Were we to draw a picture of the novel, it would not, I believe, bring before the reader the ladder of social and moral being that Graham Hough assigns. It would look more like a road map in which the cities and towns, joined together by countless highways and byroads, stood for people. Some of the roads are curved and smooth, like those between Emma and her father or Emma and Mrs. Weston; some are so full of obstacles that their destinations (Jane Fairfax, for example) are almost inaccessible. Mr. Weston and Miss Bates are like great indiscriminate towns from which radiate roads that join almost everyone.

As the image of a road map suggests, Highbury is a system of interdependence, a community of people all talking to one another, affecting, and changing one another: a collection of relationships. Miss Bates is emblematic of Highbury in this respect. In the words of E. M. Forster, "Miss Bates is bound by a hundred threads to Highbury. We cannot tear her away without bringing her mother too, and Jane Fairfax and Frank Churchill, and the whole of Box Hill."[2] Emma herself is as firmly connected to her world as Miss Bates. Perceived in her many relationships with others, Emma is seen as daughter, sister, sister-in-law, aunt, companion, intimate friend, new acquaintance, patroness, and bride. And each connection lets us see something new in her.

The interaction of characters in the novel is extensive and dynamic. All characters intersect in some way. In addition to all the major combinations, we witness sufficiently realized contact between Jane Fairfax and Mr. John Knightley, Mr. Weston and Mrs. Elton, Mr. Elton and Mr. John Knightley; we learn what Mr. Woodhouse thinks of Frank Churchill, what Mr. John Knightley thinks of Mr. Weston, and what Isabella thinks of Harriet. These represent brief encounters and the almost spur-of-the-moment judgments that arise from them. For example, Mr. John Knightley has only to see Mr. Elton once during his holiday visit to know that Mr. Elton is interested in Emma. As always in Jane Austen, the smallest detail of behavior can justify the most definitive judgment.

Even the more sustained relationships seem to be composed of many individual encounters and the individual judgments that arise from them. For example, the relationships between Mrs. Elton and Jane Fairfax, Frank Churchill and his foster parents, Jane Fairfax and Emma, and Harriet and Robert Martin's sister are discussed several times by different persons, and on the basis of brief incidents. When compared to the pattern of dialogue in *Pride and Prejudice*, these dialogues and judgments seem random and self-absorbed—indeed, like "real" conversations—yet not the less reliable for being so. Mr. Woodhouse's judgment upon Frank Churchill—that the young man is "not quite the thing"—is unreasonably and uncharitably founded, yet correct; and it is acknowledged with dismay by those who hear it.

The novel is like Highbury itself; there is no limit to the combinations within it, or to the combinations speculated upon. Marriage, always the first and last relationship in Jane Austen, is confirmed in six couples in the novel and predicted in many more. (Harriet and Mr. Elton, Emma and Mr. Elton, Emma and Frank Churchill, Harriet and Frank Churchill, Jane Fairfax and Mr. Dixon, Mr. Knightley and Jane Fairfax, Harriet and Mr. Knightley.) Indeed, speculation about love relationships is the basis of the novel's plot, because the heroine is herself a relentless matchmaker. Yet to catalogue all of these real or imagined connections is misleading. In its unlikely and changing combinations, the catalogue gives an impression of social irrationality, overworked variety, and exhaustive socialization. Yet no other novel has more the opposite effect: of rich, unbroken continuity, of uncluttered awareness, routine contentment, cooperation, and harmony. This effect is achieved not only because of the interdependence of Highbury, its commune-like nature, but because events and characters are likened to one another in subtle ways, like so many hues of one color. This too helps to explain the magic and magnetic appeal of *Emma*; we are transfixed by the kaleidoscopic patterning of its relationships.

The similarities between Emma and Mrs. Elton are often noted. Both are preoccupied with status; each adopts another young woman as protégé and satellite; both are self-centered and therefore blind. Jane Fairfax and Emma also are compared and contrasted; Miss Bates is Jane's Mr. Woodhouse. Miss Taylor is to Emma what Emma plans to be to Harriet. Mr. Perry has his counterpart in town, Mr. Wingfield. And so on.

The similarities always have psychological meaning. Characters have a tendency to repeat the relationships they have known; for example, Emma seeks a replacement for Mrs. Weston in Harriet. Isabella Knightley finds her Mr. Perry in town, another doctor who like his counterpart parodically embodies the atavistic, maternal relationship founded on one-sided knowledge and care. Both Jane Fairfax and Frank Churchill are orphaned; their original relationships disrupted, neither has a secure prototype to follow. It is difficult for Jane Fairfax to connect with others; she feels far more isolated in the presence of her aunt, for example, than Emma does in the presence of her father. Frank, on the other hand, has no notion at all of what a relationship is, of reciprocal endeavor and trust. Unlike Jane's unwavering attachment to him, his love does not include loyalty — he not only flirts with Emma but does so to torment his fiancée. Since neither has received the education of a steady and lasting parental relationship, as Emma has, they can only form an attachment that becomes "a source of repentance and misery to each." (Because of the unvalidated status of their relationship their marriage is left waiting at the end of the novel.)

Many of the transformations, actions, and events in *Emma* take place in the form of repetitions. Emma has three enlightenments; related respectively to Mr. Elton, Frank Churchill, and Mr. Knightley, they increase in intensity yet are essentially similar. Isolated events are also replayed in a changed key; Mr. Knightley rescues Harriet at the Crown Ball in a scene of great romantic delicacy involving Emma; the next day Frank Churchill rescues Harriet from the gypsies in a burlesque version. The crudeness of the second event drowns out the delicacy of the first and prepares the way for Emma's wanton blow at Miss Bates at Box Hill. The ball scene in which Mr. Knightley performs his wonderfully unobtrusive act of kindness reverberates with suggestion. It brings Emma and Mr. Knightley together for the first time; it joins them through an act of charity in the way Emma earlier planned to join Mr. Elton and Harriet the day they visited the cottage. And the look of approval Emma sends across the dance floor that night is later matched by his silent expression of approval for Emma when she visits Miss Bates the morning after Box Hill. The most resonant instance of transformation as repetition in Jane Austen, of course, is marriage. The three marriages that close the novel are different yet similar, repetitive of one another and of the marriages in the beginning of the novel. The rich overlay of experience, the almost Shakespearean imaginative continuity of the novel, is all but hypnotizing.

Because *Emma* is a novel about relationships and their natures, the "action" of the work is a dialectic. Every relationship in the novel has its unique dialectical rhythm; even the smoothest relationships encounter snags, such as the near-argument between Mr. Woodhouse and Emma about the treatment of brides. The novel's humor is almost always centered on the surprise creation of a dialectic through the sudden juxtaposition of unlikely personalities. The conversation between Mr. Knightley and Mrs. Elton about the picnic at Donwell Abbey, one of the most amusing exchanges in English fiction, does not perform at all; the humor lies in the contrast of character and is available to those who see it.

Such moments border on farce because of the deadly seriousness of the characters themselves. And Mr. Knightley, the most serious of all, is not exempted from the farce of the situation; the contrast is not available to his subjective standpoint.

Three major dialectics in the novel involve Emma herself: the interior dialectic, of which only Emma is aware; the dialectic between Emma and Mr. Knightley; and the dialectic between Emma and Highbury. By the close of the novel they all seem to become the same dialectic. They are never resolved, only validated, in marriage; the only truth is the dialectic itself. Part of the novel's greatness is that it never moves to the death of total resolution.

Emma's personality opens like a fan before us. Seen in her innumerable relationships with others, she alters continually and gracefully, and the novel is deliberately paced to allow this. Mr. Woodhouse's daughter is not Harriet's patroness or Mr. John Knightley's sister-in-law. The Emma who condescends to Harriet, self-satisfied, smirking, and dictatorial, is not the Emma we see with Mr. Knightley, witty, open, and daring. And although she is tied by countless social relations, she is neither overshadowed nor borne down by them. We cannot think of her as we do some nineteenth-century heroines, changing under circumstances like Darwinian organisms. Emma's inner nature, her stability as Emma, even as she is drawn this way and that—spoiled, criticized, disappointed, insulted, and loved—never alters; she is still Emma. Protean, elusive, capable of true goodness and deliberate cruelty, she is what she is—a reservoir of indeterminacy. She represents the genuine triumph of volition, for she is free to be better than she knows herself to be. She is faultless not in spite of her faults, but because of them.

Always doing "more than she wished and less than she ought" Emma is frequently divided between two impulses in her interior dialogue. There is a struggle, but never a war. In questioning her own treatment of the Martins, of Harriet, of Jane Fairfax, and of Miss Bates, she has some unsettling moments, yet her disposition is to like and accept herself wholeheartedly. Even after her most crucial, most soul-searching enlightenment, her final admission of her despicable treatment of Harriet, she swings back to a tolerably self-supporting state of mind. At length she begins to learn to treat others as generously as she treats herself, to accept the faultlessness of human interactions in spite of their faults. Emma's interior struggle is never laid to rest; the only resolution consists in trying to be better: "the only source whence anything like consolation or composure could be drawn, was in the resolution of her own better conduct" (*E*, p. 423). She never ceases to be one Emma and begins to be another.

Mr. Knightley, in his relation to Emma, takes the side of her that does or should do what she "ought". When she paints Harriet taller than she really is, only Mr. Knightley and this side of Emma acknowledge that she is doing it. Mr. Knightley seems to bring out the best in Emma; he makes her defend her right to be Emma, and in defending it, she becomes witty and challenging. "I shall not scold you. I leave you to your own reflections," says Mr. Knightley. "Can you trust me with such flatterers?" replies Emma (p. 330). The tension between Emma and Mr. Knightley is as vital as that in a love affair in a novel by D. H. Lawrence. From their first words to each other, every encounter between them vibrates with their unique awareness of one another, their mutual knowledge disguised under apparent differences: " 'You have made her too tall, Emma,' said Mr. Knightley. Emma knew that she had, but would not own it" (*E*, p. 48). And the secret knowledge of the other's character is not limited to Mr. Knightley. When he arrives at the Coles', Emma can tell he has come in his carriage and says:

> "There is always a look of consciousness or bustle when people come in a way which they know to be beneath them. You think you carry it off very well, I dare say, but with you it is a sort of bravado, an air of affected unconcern; I always observe it whenever I meet you under those circumstances. *Now* you have nothing to try for. You are not afraid of being supposed ashamed. You are not striving to look taller than any body else. *Now* I shall be very happy to walk in the same room with you."
> "Nonsensical girl!" was his reply, but not at all in anger.
> (*E,* pp. 213-214)

Such encounters suggest an immediacy of awareness and intimacy that is undeniably sexual. There are no sexual "overtones" in *Emma*; the sexuality is there, in the minds and speech and emotional intensity of the characters, in the mental urgency of every encounter. The scene at the Crown Ball when Mr. Knightley asks the defenseless and snubbed Harriet to dance is alive with the sense of a new understanding between Emma and Mr. Knightley. Until the end of the chapter, no words are spoken between them; like the love in *Persuasion*, their love is silent. Eye contact replaces speech: "her countenance said much, as soon as she could catch his eye again" (*E*, p. 328). And the wonderfully powerful: "her eyes invited him irresistibly to come to her and be thanked" (p. 330). One feels that this is what being in love is about, not all the talk, planning, and invention Emma imagines it is. It is the power to move, to know the other person.

The Crown Ball is a scene of extraordinary delicacy and love. Set off by the benevolent hum of Miss Bates's monologue, its strength lies in Emma's watching Mr. Knightley perform this act of kindness; her appreciation of it makes her a better Emma than the Emma who mistreats the Martins, the Emma who is above everyone. And Mr. Knightley, who would do what he does now for any woman in the novel, does it here for Emma, as they both know. The dialogue that follows registers the new intimacy with spirit, and without losing a sense of their individuality. The scene ends in dance:

> "Will you? said he, offering his hand.
> "Indeed I will. You have shown that you can dance, and you know we are not really so much brother and sister as to make it at all improper."
> "Brother and sister! no, indeed." (*E*, pp. 330-331)

Mr. Knightley knows he loves Emma at this point; characteristically, Emma does not yet know she loves him. But the reader is not ignorant and his knowledge gives the scene its exquisite emotion.

The scene is surrounded and intertwined with contrasts that set off its romantic delicacy. Preceded by Mr. Weston's indiscriminate hospitality, Frank Churchill's nervousness, and the Eltons' sneering self-importance, Mr. Knightley's act suddenly crystallizes the three concerned—himself, Harriet, and Emma—in a brilliant

tableau. Miss Bates's interpolated monologue is a wonderful contrast to the delicate discriminations of the event. It is as though
their love were founded in her jumbled benevolence.

The chapter itself is framed on one side by Emma's private admission of an entirely deflated interest in Frank Churchill, and on
the other by Frank Churchill's mock-heroic rescue of Harriet,
pointedly used to establish the real heroism of Mr. Knightley's
action. The ball scene in *Emma* is flanked by events that, through
contrasts, set off its intensity and validate its sincerity.

It seems to me that in this respect *Emma* is a great novel about
"the association of man and woman" — to use T. S. Eliot's phrase.
Emma and Mr.Knightley actually make each other larger, more
interesting. Without Mr. Knightley, Emma is a self-satisfied busy-
body; without Emma, Mr. Knightley is a dull and predictable
English gentlemen. Emma is responsible for Mr. Knightley's one
unpredictable act in the entire novel, his standing up Mr. Elton
one morning. Infuriated, Mr. Elton recalls: "I met William Lar-
kins . . . as I got near the house, and he told me I should not find
his master at home, but I did not believe him. — William seemed
rather out of humour. He did not know what was come of his
master lately, he said" (p. 458). Because each has always possessed
a part of the other, the marriage between Emma and Mr. Knightley does not wrench either from an old identity into a new one.
They do not seek to annihilate one another — the way, for example, part of Edmund Bertram is annihilated when he marries
Fanny. Emma is still Emma and Mr. Knightley still Mr. Knightley; Emma even wishes to continue to call him so. The only real
difference is the knowledge of love between them, and the willingness to be influenced by the other that, as always, is central to Jane
Austen's conception of love. After reading Mr. John Knightley's
response to his brother's announcement of his engagement, Emma
says:

> "He writes like a sensible man . . . I honour his sincerity. It
> is very plain that he considers the good fortune of the engage-
> ment as all on my side . . . "
> "My Emma, he means no such thing. He only means . . ."

"He and I should differ very little in our estimation of the two,"—interrupted she, with a sort of serious smile—"much less, perhaps, than he is aware of . . . "

"Emma, my dear Emma—"

"Oh!" she cried with more thorough gaiety, "if you fancy your brother does not do me justice, only wait till my dear father is in the secret, and hear his opinion. Depend upon it, he will be much farther from doing *you* justice." (*E*, p. 464)

Here is the old Emma, asserting herself with the same archness and self-love, yet this time, with something new added—a kind of self-irony. "Oh! I always deserve the best treatment, because I never put up with any other" (*E*, p. 474).

Each wishes to make the other more like his or her self; yet each loves that part of the other that is not similar. This rapport between Emma and Mr. Knightley is, I believe, more central to the novel than Graham Hough's hierarchy of characters. Hough distinguishes five kinds of discourse in the novel and asserts that the "objective narrative" with its Johnsonian vocabulary and thoughtful, well-ordered, analytical generalizing sets "the standard by which all the rest is measured."[3] Since Mr. Knightley's speech assimilates the objective narrative most completely, he is the highest on an unequivocal moral scale: "Mr. Knightley, who is never wrong, maintains this style of sober moral evaluation more consistently than anyone else . . . In his presence, conversation is always lifted from the familiar and the anecdotal to the level of general reflection; the characters become types; and the actual persons around him assume the air of personae in a moral apologue."[4] Hough gives as an example Mr. Knightley's comments concerning Mrs. Elton and Jane Fairfax: "Another thing must be taken into consideration too—Mrs. Elton does not talk to Miss Fairfax as she speaks of her. We all know the differences between the pronouns he or she and thou, the plainest spoken amongst us; we all feel the influence of something beyond common civility in our personal intercourse with each other—a something more early implanted . . . And besides the operation of this as a general principle you may be sure that Miss Fairfax awes Mrs. Elton by her superiority both of mind and manner; and that face to face Mrs. Elton treats her with all the respect which she has a claim to" (*E*, pp. 286-287). Yet Mr. Knightley's words simply are not true in the very example Hough gives. Mrs. Elton is irrepressible, so much so that she almost usurps the closing lines of the novel. Although we never see her alone with Jane Fairfax, we know from the liberties taken in finding Jane a position that Mrs. Elton's private behavior is as bold and intrusive as her public behavior. If Mrs. Elton is not awed by the "superiority both of mind and manner" of Mr. Knightley, who as Hough says is superior to all, she will not be awed by Jane Fairfax. Mr. Knightley is wrong in his evaluation here, as he is in his optimistic insistence that, were Frank Churchill to act more virtuously toward his father, his foster parents would bend and respect him for it. Mr. Knightley is a pastoral figure who insists on seeing the "actual persons" around him as "personae in a moral apologue." This is not the way Jane Austen views the world, nor can it be the vision she really supports. As Mary Ellmann has said, the endorsement of moral stolidity is reluctant, qualified by Mr. Knightley's pleasure in Emma's defects: "I am losing all my bitterness against spoilt children, my dearest Emma. I who am owing all my happiness to *you*, would it not be horrible ingratitude in me to be severe on them?" (*E*, p. 461).[5] The weight of the novel is centered not in Mr. Knightley but in Emma, or in the contributing tension between them.

Mr. Knightley is the link between Emma's interior struggle and her struggle with Highbury. He seems to represent both her conscience and the community. Almost every time Emma sets herself against her conscience, she is also setting herself against Mr. Knightley and against the values of Highbury. (Her treatment of Robert Martin is the best example of this opposition.) Emma's interior coordination, her quest to know and approve of herself, is solidly linked to her exterior coordination, or her arrival at a juster relation to others and to the community.

Essays on *Emma* have a tendency to describe Highbury the way an ethnographer writes history, sorting through the picked bones of institutions and beliefs. The inner consistency, the living society, escapes attention. Class divisions and difficulties are stressed, and moral traits are eventually viewed as possessions of a particu-

lar class, or class attitude. I do not intend to decry this view, but
pursued too far, it reduces the society of Highbury to a sack of
struggling types in some manner creating order out of chaos. It is
not the Highbury Emma sees standing on the doorstep of Ford's
one morning:

> Mr. Perry walking hastily by, Mr. William Cox letting him-
> self in at the office door, Mr. Cole's carriage horses returning
> from exercise, or a stray letter-boy on an obstinate mule,
> were the liveliest objects she could presume to expect; and
> when her eyes fell only on the butcher with his tray, a tidy old
> woman travelling homewards from shop with her full basket,
> two curs quarrelling over a dirty bone, and a string of daw-
> dling children round the baker's little bow-window eyeing the
> gingerbread, she knew she had no reason to complain, and
> was amused enough; quite enough still to stand at the door.
> (*E*, p. 233)

Highbury, it is true, is made up of classes and their individual
members. Yet however different the traits of personality and class,
they are taken into a functioning society and reshaped by inner
organizing forces. Miss Bates is perhaps the nearest symbol of
Highbury; all classes join and cooperate in her, just as all gossip
passes through her vacant mind. She is the repository of all that
occurs and has occurred in Highbury. Her small apartment joins
the older gentry (the Woodhouses and Knightleys), the new rich
(the Coles), and the lower-middle to lower-class townspeople and
clerks. She represents Highbury's fluidity and mobility, its tolerance of past and future classes, or part of the sensibility that helped
England avoid a French Revolution.

Emma sets herself against this Highbury, as she does finally
against Miss Bates at Box Hill. After every disagreement with Mr.
Knightley she visits Miss Bates, as though humbly paying deference to Highbury itself. She does not like visiting Miss Bates for
the very reason she should visit her: because it sanctions class fluidity. She does not wish to fall in with the "second and third rate of
Highbury"; she wishes to have her own "set." Her greatest sin in
the novel is cutting off Harriet's warm attachment to the Martins;
as Lionel Trilling has said, she is a reactionary, out to stop social

mobility. And Jane Austen gives her snobbery deliberately vindictive overtones: "The regular and best families Emma could hardly suppose [the Coles] would presume to invite—neither Donwell, nor Hartfield, nor Randalls. Nothing should tempt her to go, if they did; and she regretted that her father's known habits would be giving her refusal less meaning than she could wish" (*E*, p. 207). If anything saves Emma after such deliberate unkindness, it is that she actually wants to, and does, go to the Coles' dinner. At bottom, Emma is the most social person in the novel: totally preoccupied with and loving all her relationships with people. This is the basis of the contrast between her and Jane Fairfax, who is a solitary, and who, in her marriage to a morally and intellectually inferior person, will continue to be a solitary.

One of the many ironies surrounding Emma's social preferences is that she will not admit the "true gentility" of Robert Martin, documented by the simple dignity of his written proposal to Harriet and his behavior to her after she refuses him, and yet will sit through an evening of "everyday remarks, dull repetitions, old news, and heavy jokes" at the Coles' and decide them to be "worthy people, who deserved to be made happy" (*E*, p. 231). The reason for the contradiction lies in the conclusion to this quotation: "And left a name behind that would not soon die away" (*E*, p. 231). What Emma requires of her inferior acquaintances is that they aggrandize her. In her comment about Robert Martin she makes this clear: "The yeomanry are precisely the order of people with whom I feel I can have nothing to do. A degree or two lower, and a creditable appearance might interest me; I might hope to be useful to their families in some way or other. But a farmer can need none of my help, and is therefore in one sense as much above my notice as in every other he is below it" (*E*, p. 29). And we see the self-serving nature of her patronage of the lower class when she visits the sick cottager.

Emma's charity visit has undergone many interpretations, and almost always appears in any discussion of Jane Austen's class attitudes. In trying to answer the question of *Emma*'s relevance to us today, Arnold Kettle points out that it is not necessary for a novelist writing in Jane Austen's time to suggest a solution to the problem of class divisions and prejudice, but that it is morally necessary for the author to notice the existence of the problem. Jane Austen, he decides, fails to do so:

> The values and standards of the Hartfield world are based on the assumption that it is right and proper for a minority of the community to live at the expense of the majority. No amount of sophistry can get away from this fact and to discuss the moral concern of Jane Austen without facing it would be hypocrisy. It is perfectly true that, within the assumptions of aristocratic society, the values recommended in *Emma* are sensitive enough. Snobbery, smugness, condescension, lack of consideration, unkindness of any description, are held up to our disdain. But the fundamental condescension, the basic unkindness which permits the sensitive values of *Emma* to be applicable only to one person in ten or twenty, is this not left unscathed? Is there not here a complacency which renders the hundred little incomplacencies almost irrelevant?[6]

This is highly persuasive criticism of *Emma*, and Kettle is right in saying that "no amount of sophistry" can disguise the fundamental questions it raises. Yet it persuades us mainly because the writer is so sure of his moral stance—most literary criticism is far more slippery—and because that stance happens to be a particularly appealing one. The moral judgment made against *Emma* is disturbingly simple. First of all, there are no "aristocrats" in the novel; even the Churchills are just inflated gentry. Nor does Jane Austen view the landed class in the novel as parasitic; she sees it as a functioning part of a changing organism. Mr. Knightley manages his land, has little cash, and has a younger brother who makes a living as a lawyer. Emma's destiny as a woman—to be spoiled, overprotected, given a weak, trivial education, and then left to her own devices—is hardly to be envied. And the social world of the novel is peopled with upwardly and downwardly mobile individuals. It is viewed not from the perspective of frozen class division but from a perspective of living change. It is not France in the 1780s but England at the beginning of the nineteenth century.

Kettle's interpretation of the scene of Emma's visit to the sick cottager forms the basis of his argument; it is in this particular scene that the moral issue is "shelved," that the existence of the problem is unrecognized. Yet while he notes the irony of Emma's remarks upon leaving the cottage, his conclusions rest exclusively upon the visit and its aftermath. Emma's words before she arrives at the cottage are equally significant. Having told Harriet she will never marry, Emma explains why her own spinsterhood could never make her ridiculous:

> Never mind, Harriet, I shall not be a poor old maid; and it is poverty only which makes celibacy contemptible to a generous public! A single woman, with a very narrow income, must be a ridiculous, disagreeable, old maid! the proper sport of boys and girls; but a single woman, of good fortune, is always respectable, and may be as sensible and pleasant as anybody else. And the distinction is not quite so much against the candour and common sense of the world as appears at first; for a very narrow income has a tendency to contract the mind, and sour the temper. Those who can barely live, and who live perforce in a very small, and generally very inferior, society, may well be illiberal and cross. (*E*, p. 85)

The exaggerated expressions and conceited ironies of Emma's speech are characteristic of her conversation in Harriet's company. If Mr. Knightley's skepticism makes her witty, Harriet's servile awe makes her unreasonable. When asked, as they near the cottage, if she knows Jane Fairfax, Emma replies:

> Oh! yes; we are always forced to be acquainted whenever she comes to Highbury. By the bye, *that* is almost enough to put one out of conceit with a niece. Heaven forbid! at least, that I should ever bore people half so much about all the Knightleys together, as she does about Jane Fairfax. One is sick of the very name of Jane Fairfax. Every letter from her is read forty times over; her compliments to all friends go round and round again; and if she does but send her aunt the pattern of a stomacher, or knit a pair of garters for her grandmother, one hears of nothing else for a month. I wish Jane Fairfax very well; but she tires me to death. (*E*, p. 86)

The poverty that Emma speaks of in the first quotation and the sickness she feels in hearing about Jane Fairfax find their counterparts in the real "sickness and poverty . . . which she came to visit." The contempt Emma really feels for the poor is very clear in the first speech (poor and elderly spinsters are "the proper sport of boys and girls"); her willingness to allow them to be "illiberal and cross" is an extension of her contempt. In the cottage this attitude is elaborated: "She understood their ways, could allow for their ignorance and their temptations, had no romantic expectations of extraordinary virtue from those, for whom education had done so little" (E, p. 86). Emma's "allowance" for ignorance and temptation is no more than an assumption of them. Even after reading Robert Martin's letter, we recall, she still insists that he is ignorant. The snapping bitterness of her tirade against Jane Fairfax, who is less fortunate than herself and who will have to earn a living, is enough to prove that even the rich can be illiberal and cross: "One is sick of the very name of Jane Fairfax . . . I wish Jane Fairfax very well; but she tires me to death." When such an example of Emma's compassion is followed with "They were now approaching the cottage, and all idle topics were superseded. Emma was very compassionate" (E, p. 86), the irony is so obvious that I question Kettle's interpretation that the moral issue is being shelved. The self-satisfied feeling Emma derives from the visit culminates when, upon seeing Mr. Elton, she says, "Well, (smiling) I hope it may be allowed that if compassion has produced exertion and relief to the sufferers, it has done all that is truly important. If we feel for the wretched, enough to do all we can for them, the rest is empty sympathy, only distressing to ourselves" (E, p. 87). Once again, the reappearance of a single word, in this case "distressing," makes us aware of the gap between Emma's real and spoken intentions. Even the "distresses of the poor" finally disappear into "what is distressing to ourselves."

It is precisely the moral issue then that is being put forward, put forward on the most demanding level: the practical, individual level. What is being subordinated to it is the collective issue, or the theoretical view of conduct as an expression of class. Such a view would let Emma off the hook, would make her class more responsible for her attitude than her own being. For all Jane Austen's awareness of the effect of class on character, she is never naive enough to overlook the existence of individual volition. She would not have written off the "little incomplacencies" as readily as Kettle does. To Austen's view, the "hundred little incomplacencies" make life tolerable for everyone; are we not required to imagine the effects of Emma's complacency on Robert Martin and his family? Emma is wrong to snub the Martins, and to encourage Harriet to snub them, not because as a class the yeomanry deserve to rise, but because she aims to break a moral and emotional tie between Harriet and the Martins that has already formed. It is on this level, the level of individual practice, that social damage is incurred in Jane Austen. From this point of view Kettle's broad class complacency is an abstraction, an evasion. Changes in the quality of social life originate on the concrete, atomized level.

Emma herself learns this lesson in the course of the novel. Indeed, it is her first lesson, because until she recognizes her own immediate effect on others, on Harriet and the Martins and Miss Bates, until she actually experiences her tie to a community of others, all talk about social responsibility and class difference is lost on her. In *Emma,* Austen makes us see the primary obstacles to class consciousness.

Emma's feelings toward her social inferiors are governed not so much by an unwillingness to see, converse with, or help them as by an insistence on regulating their lives. She does not wish to participate in Highbury society unless she can lead, on the dance floor and elsewhere. In essence she wishes not to cooperate but to rule, as Frank Churchill's mock proclamations at Box Hill suggest. Miss Bates offends her because she is uncontrollable; Emma cannot stop or even regulate the flow of her boring remarks. The urge to control is the basis of her insult at Box Hill: Miss Bates's dull remarks must be "limited as to number—only three at once" (*E,* p. 370).

It is important to Emma to feel that Highbury needs her but that she does not need Highbury. She imagines herself the envy and idol of all her social inferiors: young Robert Martin "will connect himself well if he can" (*E,* p. 50); and the Coles' main object in giving the dinner is to see Emma at their table. At every social event Emma sees herself as giving the honor rather than as possibly receiving it. E. M. Forster's remark is appropriate to her: for some, it is perhaps better to receive than to give.

Emma's unwillingness to mix with Highbury has a personal analogue in her wish to remain single. Both reveal the same superior tendency to remain aloof, to oversee life without participating in it. Her first realization of love is appropriately attended by the first realization of her need for human society generally:

> The child to be born at Randall's must be a tie there even dearer than herself; and Mrs. Weston's heart and time would be occupied by it. They should lose her; and, probably, in great measure, her husband also. — Frank Churchill would return among them no more; and Miss Fairfax, it was reasonable to suppose, would soon cease to belong to Highbury. They would be married, and settled either at or near Enscombe. All that were good would be withdrawn; and if to these losses, the loss of Donwell were to be added, what would remain of cheerful or of rational society within their reach? Mr. Knightley to be no longer coming there for his evening comfort! — No longer walking in at all hours, as if ever willing to change his own home for their's! — How was it to be endured? (*E*, p. 422)

A great deal of the force of Emma's realization of love lies in the implicit recognition of dependence, of need, for another person. What astounds her is her own failure to see, year after year, the importance of Mr. Knightley's presence to her.

And once the love and need for another person is admitted, a sense of obligation naturally follows. It is significant that Emma achieves knowledge of her "heart" and knowledge of her "conduct" simultaneously: "It darted through her, with the speed of an arrow, that Mr. Knightley must marry no one but herself! . . . Her own conduct, as well as her own heart, was before her in the same few minutes. She saw it all with a clearness which had never blessed her before. How improperly had she been acting by Harriet! How inconsiderate, how indelicate, how irrational, how unfeeling had been her conduct! What blindness, what madness, had led her on!" (*E*, p. 408). Emma learns a "sense of justice" for the first time — in the words of *Mansfield Park,* a sense of "what is owed to everybody." Never in Jane Austen do we find a convenient separation between the personal and the social act. As Mr. Knightley tells Emma at Box Hill, her remark to Miss Bates—to Emma no more than a careless indulgence—is inevitably a public act: "You, whom she had known from an infant, whom she had seen grow up from a period when her notice was an honour, to have you now, in thoughtless spirits, and the pride of the moment, laugh at her, humble her—and before her niece, too—and before others, many of whom (certainly *some,*) would be entirely guided by *your* treatment of her" (*E,* p. 375).

The scene at Box Hill possesses great emotional intensity. Each time we read it—no matter how objective familiarity or reason may have made us—Emma's cruelty completely shocks us. There is something particularly moving and frightening about the rejection of the comic figure in art, such as the rejection of Falstaff or of a clown in a Charlie Chaplin film. Miss Bates's emotional vulnerability, her blind (indeed her comic) goodness in expecting others to be as simply affectionate as herself, gives the scene its special pathos. And however Mr. Knightley finally stresses Miss Bates's social vulnerability, his speech begins with the frankly appalled question, "How could you be so unfeeling to Miss Bates?"

Yet the lack of feeling is not what makes the scene so shocking. Emma's action violates the most basic human law found in any society whether barbarous or advanced: the protection of the weak. Miss Bates is defenseless, as the first description of her makes clear: "She had not intellectual superiority to make atonement to herself, or to frighten those who might hate her, into outward respect" (*E,* p. 21). What leads Emma to mistreat her? We cannot really answer this question any more than we can explain an act of violence in an absurdist work. It is hot; Emma is tired of herself and of Frank Churchill; she is bored; and her discontent flowers with terrifying naturalness into cruelty.

Emma delivers the insult because she "could not resist." And the remarkable impact of the scene comes from our understanding her action though we know it to be wrong. We understand it not through its overt causes—Emma's impatience and boredom, her exasperated attempt to entertain herself since no one else will entertain her—but through its covert reality: there is no reason for it; it is simply a case of unrestrained human hostility. In this moment, perhaps more than in any other moment in Jane Austen, it is impossible to entertain D. W. Harding's notion of the "social detachment" that arises from having to restrain ourselves in society; indeed, only through restraint do the characters achieve a modicum of "social engagement." It is through resisting these irresistible impulses and hostilities that people in Austen's society can maintain a tolerably open atmosphere for the individual. Where, finally, do Emma's "honesty" and "sincerity" place Miss Bates but in a condition of social estrangement? Emma's famous cruelty takes place in the open air of Box Hill (itself a contradiction in terms), in a "natural" environment away from the home community. This choice of setting gives us a rather pointed indication of Jane Austen's opinion of human nature, of how human beings behave when the muzzle is off. To Jane Austen, nothing boxes the individual in more tightly than his own craving for freedom.

Unlike Emma, Mr. Knightley has, in his own words, the "English delicacy toward the feelings of other people" (*E*, p. 149), as his protection of the slow-witted and defenseless Harriet reveals. In his conversation with Mrs. Elton, Mr. Knightley states his understanding of human behavior, and we observe one of the most richly ambivalent problems in Jane Austen realizing itself.

> "It is to be a morning scheme, you know, Knightley; quite a simple thing. I shall wear a large bonnet, and bring one of my little baskets hanging on my arm. Here,—probably this basket with pink ribbon. And Jane will have such another. There is to be no form or parade—a sort of gipsy party.—We are to walk about your gardens, and gather the strawberries ourselves, and sit under trees;—and whatever else you may like to provide, it is to be all out of doors—a table spread in the shade, you know. Everything as natural and simple as possible. Is not that your idea?"
>
> "Not quite. My idea of the simple and the natural will be to have the table spread in the dining-room. The nature and the simplicity of gentlemen and ladies, with their servants and

furniture, I think is best observed by meals within doors.
When you are tired of eating strawberries in the garden,
there shall be cold meat in the house." (*E*, p. 355)

Mrs. Elton's idea of a "gipsy party" is given added irony when we
consider that the real gipsy party in the novel comes close to
attacking Harriet for her money. Yet Mr. Knightley is not simply
the spokesman for Jane Austen in his comment. As his name
suggests, Mr. Knightley is a slightly anachronistic figure, and his
equating "servants" with "furniture" reveals this. His world is a
stable, pastoral world in which everything is in its place, people
have the predictable stability of furniture, and the virtuous person
is always deferred to. This is not the world of Highbury, where
gentlewomen sometimes slip to the near-servant status of
governess or even, like Miss Bates, to a barely genteel poverty;
where governesses become the mistresses of estates; where
inhumane behavior surfaces in its members; and, above all, where
an encounter of opposites like that between Mr. Knightley and
Mrs. Elton can take place.

Highbury is kept on through an endless dialectic. Like a well-
oiled machine, it runs on the cooperation and coordination of its
parts. Lionel Trilling has come closest to recognizing the basis of
cooperation of Highbury, but as I have already suggested, he is
mistaken in calling it pastoral. His argument brilliantly articulates
a modern bias, for many readers, particularly American readers,
view Jane Austen in this way. Cooperation itself is viewed as an ar-
chaic phenomenon. But to Jane Austen cooperation was no more
pastoral than the moral restrictions in the novels were mysterious
taboos. As Trilling states, the pastoral idyll excludes the idea of
activity and includes an idea of harmonic stasis.[7] Yet Highbury is
an imperfect, changing society. It functions smoothly because
almost everyone makes a constant effort to maintain it: "Some
change of countenance was necessary for each gentleman as they
walked into Mrs. Weston's drawing-room; — Mr. Elton must
compose his joyous looks, and Mr. John Knightley disperse his ill-
humour. Mr. Elton must smile less, and Mr. John Knightley more,
to fit them for the place" (*E*, p. 117). These accomodations are

minor compared to the continual exertion required of almost all
to abide the slowness of Mr. Woodhouse and the loquacity of Miss
Bates. I cannot agree with Trilling that everyone except Emma,
the "modern" personality, experiences only their charm and
goodness. Mr. Knightley must strain to be heard by both, and
Jane Fairfax's despair is haunting: "Oh! . . . the comfort of being
sometimes alone!" (*E*, p. 363). Mr. Woodhouse and Miss Bates are
both loved *and* tolerated. Similarly, Mr. Knightley's willingness to
move to Hartfield does not assume a lack of will. He is the hero of
Emma because his move *is* a sacrifice.

Highbury, like all the communities in Jane Austen, is conceived
as possessing an almost personal identity and will. "Frank Churchill was looked on as sufficiently belonging to the place to make
his merit and prospects a kind of common concern" (*E*, p. 17).
"By birth [Jane Fairfax] belonged to Highbury" (*E*, p. 163). Like
Meryton in *Pride and Prejudice*, Highbury ingests and rejects
materials that come into it; be it John Knightley's sullenness or
Emma's energy, that trait is reworked in such a manner that when
it reappears as part of the social body it has been molded to fit a
larger purpose. It has become part of the network of influences
that, through checks and balances, ensure Highbury's survival. In
Emma, this process does not reduce the human spirit but expands
it; the efforts required of all its members make them better
people. The atmosphere of "intelligent love" — when it dominates — is well earned. Many of the dialogues seem to pull and
stretch under the strain of accommodation: Emma's little dis-
agreements with her father, Mr. Knightley's conversation with
Miss Bates, even Mr. Weston's exchange with Mrs. Elton about his
son. At moments the intelligent and sensitive person is forced into
irony, and this irony is not a form of social detachment but a form
of social adjustment. It is not like the superior sarcasm of Mr.
Palmer in *Sense and Sensibility*, which is treated with astringent
disapproval. When used sincerely, irony is a benevolent compromise: a way of maintaining social integrity without sacrificing
personal integrity, as Emma's first conversation with Mrs. Elton
reveals. Such irony is, on the simplest level, courtesy; it is also a
method of comprehending reality. In a world where, for reasons

beyond the control of the intelligence of the characters, "seldom
. . . does complete truth belong to any human disclosure," irony is
a more truthful and humble mode of comprehension than direct
statement.

Many critics have pointed out that no one works in *Emma*. Yet
everyone is working, morally and psychically, to sustain this
cooperative enterprise of civilized living. As in *Mansfield Park*, a
certain amount of sheer psychic energy is required to make the
social order endure. This is difficult for us to fathom, for the
modern reader inevitably looks upon inactivity as stagnation; Mil-
ton's Adam and Eve in the Garden of Eden before their fall seem
to us like old-age pensioners. In *Emma,* those who contribute relatively little to the cooperative enterprise, John Knightley and Jane
Fairfax, are either involved or preparing to be involved in the
working world. John Knightley has always seemed to me a curiously modern type, a commuting professional man who divides his
time entirely between work and family. He and Jane Fairfax lack
the energy for Highbury, and through them Austen registers the
effect that the breakup of a ruling, or leisure, class will have on re-
fined and civilized values. Austen knew that a community like
Highbury could be maintained only if its members took a constant, unflagging interest in one another's welfare. Emma herself
instinctively acknowledges this when, upon noticing that Jane
Fairfax is not very curious about the news of Mr. Elton's marriage,
she remarks, "You are silent, Miss Fairfax—but I hope you mean
to take an interest in this news" (*E,* p. 175). Like much of Austen's
dialogue, even the most offhand comments join in the underlying
continuity of the work.

Marriage in *Emma* signifies the validation, not the resolution,
of the different dialectics. Frank Churchill's character, Mr.
Knightley asserts, "will improve" after his marriage. And as Emma
and Mr. Knightley continue to retain their separate identities, we
anticipate that cooperation and compromise will maintain the
relationship. Emma has had three enlightenments, and we expect
that she will experience more.

Mr. Knightley sets the pattern of compromise by moving to
Hartfield, an action antithetical to modern ideas of marriage. Yet

since the most serious sin in the novel is Emma's insistence that Harriet cut the Martins in order to preserve her own friendship, it follows that Mr. Knightley should not commit a similar unkindness in making Emma give up her father for him. Since he has no really important relationship to give up in leaving his estate, the sacrifice is proper. Perhaps more significantly, Mr. Knightley's move to Hartfield marks the first time in a Jane Austen novel in which the relationship begins to take precedence over the "place" or estate. Could we imagine Darcy moving to Longbourn? It is also a subtly feminist praise of Mr. Knightley, whose practical sensibility does not include the traditional masculine insistence that his future wife leave her family to become Mrs. Knightley, the mistress of Donwell.

Jane Austen was interested in the stability of form, in what kept the great basic plans of social organization, one of which is marriage, so steadfast throughout whole epochs. To say that this concern is outdated — as several of Austen's critics have reluctantly concluded — reveals a curious misconception. Most people marry, and almost everyone participates in some way in the larger institutions of our society. Yet it has been the preoccupation of a post-Darwinian age to see struggle as the natural state of things and therefore to judge a novelist who explores the implications of our cooperative history as somehow blind or narrow or even trivial.

Why, one may ask, in a novel about social cooperation, is an individual, and a willful individual at that, so undeniably the main subject? Why is the novel not called *Highbury*? The novel as written could not be called *Highbury*; it is clearly a tribute to this heroine whom the author mistakenly thought "no one but myself will much like." Emma even threatens to take control over the work and write her own novel about Harriet: to give her a family history, a personality, beauty and stature, a love affair, a husband, and a social position. This deference to Emma, to her creative impulse, registers the author's interest in the individual person, for whom, after all, society was organized to begin with. Those who forget this origin by placing an abstract social ambition above it — General Tilney, Mrs. Ferrars, Lady Catherine de Bourgh, Sir Walter Elliot — are never contemplated without disapproval. Emma reminds us of what Highbury is for; while she has not the right to remain aloof from it, she has the right to be dissatisfied with it.

Emma is based on a recognition of the life of the individual as a functioning whole that must be coordinated internally before it can function externally. Those who do not coordinate internally — more simply, those, like Harriet, who never know themselves — become the willing victims of those exterior forces that, because they never see them, will always control them. When Arnold Kettle says that the sensitive values of *Emma* are available to one in twenty, he is being generous. They are available to even fewer than that, not even to Emma until the end of the novel. They are available mainly to the intelligent, and only partially to the less intelligent. One does not have to be intelligent to be good in Jane Austen, but one does have to be intelligent to be free, to see and evaluate one's choices. Partly for this reason, an Austen novel seems inexorable beside most Dickens novels. Often in Dickens, in order to be good — above all to be a good woman — one has to be simple-minded. Jane Austen makes us acknowledge the undemocratic truth that those who are born unintelligent are at a terrible disadvantage in the world. Her belief in the importance of education, one of her most constant and serious concerns, is an extension of this awareness.

This is all the more reason why in *Emma* Jane Austen insists on the necessity and finally the benevolence of social cooperation: because it alone protects the Harriets and the Miss Bateses of the world, cares for, tolerates, and loves them. "She must laugh at such a close! Such an end of the doleful disappointments of five weeks back! Such a heart! — such a Harriet!" (*E*, p. 475). *Emma* is a novel of human interdependence in every sense. It is Harriet who makes Emma accomplished, Mr. Knightley who makes her witty, Jane Fairfax who makes her average, and, in the closing lines, Mrs. Elton who makes her tasteful:

> The wedding was very much like other weddings, where the parties have no taste for finery or parade; and Mrs. Elton, from the particulars detailed by her husband, thought it all

extremely shabby, and very inferior to her own. — "Very little white satin, very few lace veils; a most pitiful business! — Selina would stare when she heard of it." — But, in spite of these deficiencies, the wishes, the hopes, the confidence, the predictions of the small band of true friends who witnessed the ceremony, were fully answered in the perfect happiness of the union. (*E*, p. 484)

"In spite of these deficiencies" may be read "because of these deficiencies." In a world that indiscriminately blesses the marriages of Mr. and Mrs. Elton and Harriet and Robert Martin, the union between Emma and Mr. Knightley is surely one of "perfect happiness." We understand them through comparison.

6

The Radical Pessimism
of *Persuasion*

A gentleman and a lady are traveling in a hired coach up a rough lane in Sussex, around the year 1817. Their destination is a place called Willingden. The driver grumbles and shakes his shoulders at having to pursue so difficult a side-road, and — as if to justify his complaints — the carriage overturns. After scrambling out, the gentleman discovers that he has sprained his foot. The laborers from a nearby hayfield gather around to watch, and a gentleman approaches, introduces himself, and offers assistance. In the course of their conversation, it is discovered that the travelers have reached a parish called Willingden, but that it is not the Willingden they are seeking. After much confusion, they learn that there are two places by that name in the same county.

Whatever we associate with the novels of Jane Austen, we do not expect them to begin like this, yet the above is a summary of the opening of Austen's last, unfinished novel, *Sanditon*. The gentleman who sprains his foot is a capitalist speculator traveling with his wife, and the ensuing chapters are filled with restless dialogue concerning his efforts to turn his home village, Sanditon, into a profitable seaside resort. This alone would strike us as uncharacteristic of the author's concerns, but the opening itself is even more so. The scene opens in the homeless universe of travel and ends in an atmosphere of almost complete geographic disorientation — a disorientation made even more uncomfortable by the experience of physical injury. The main characters appear to be placed in an open social frame, for the carriage driver and field workers are not shadows (as in Austen's earlier novels) but distinct presences. The manuscript looks curiously like the beginning of a Victorian novel, and not just because of the Dickensian carriage driver and the roving capitalist. The discovery of the two Willingdens is ominous. The world had grown just large enough to contain two parishes of the same name; between 1801 and 1831 the population of England increased from roughly eleven to sixteen and a half million; new towns were built, and old localities grew and split and doubled. Austen's scene of human, humorous confusion may be one of the first expressions in English fiction of the modern anxiety of displacement. Just as science fiction writers play on our fear of infinity by creating other worlds, modern novelists use mistaken locations and identities to convey the dread of endless anonymity. Later in *Sanditon*, the possibility of another coincidence is entertained: that two families, of the same size and means and taste in remote resorts, might bear the same name.

Sanditon may seem an oblique entrance into a discussion of *Persuasion*, but it is a telling one. If *Sanditon* had been finished, the common belief in Jane Austen's separation from the Victorians would never have taken hold; and no other novel has suffered more from this notion than *Persuasion*. The traditional assumption that all the novels are essentially the same in their unambitious, un-Victorian concern with domesticity is highly questionable without *Sanditon*, but a completed *Sanditon* would have precluded its formation. The social frame of *Sanditon* is sufficiently precarious. The heroine herself is a stranger in a foreign county, introduced to strangers; and the world she finds herself in would have rivaled Thackeray in its exposure of what society is like "when Rich People are Sordid" (*Sanditon*, p. 402). The story even includes a tender, half mulatto heiress who is to be forced on an improverished baronet. And this is the novel that was begun only a few months after the completion of *Persuasion*.

A closer look at *Persuasion* will prove that the difference is not extreme, for many of the conceptual changes apparent in the unfinished work also exist in the finished one. *Persuasion* is Jane Austen's most "modern" work—perhaps the only novel that fully justifies F. R. Leavis's placing its author at the beginning of the modern tradition. In narrative mode, social view, and character conception, it marks a radical change from all that has gone before. Its debilitating ambiguities and hatreds, its conception of society, its surrender to disgust, take us through George Eliot and

Henry James to, finally, the theories of Georg Lukács. For *Persuasion* is a novel as Lukács defined the novel: the epic of a failed world, or of the failure of the self to fulfill itself in the world.

The change in narrative style is immediately felt:

> Vanity was the beginning and the end of Sir Walter Elliot's character; vanity of person and of situation. He had been remarkably handsome in his youth; and, at fifty-four, was still a very fine man. Few women could think more of their personal appearance than he did; nor could the valet of any new made lord be more delighted with the place he held in society. He considered the blessing of beauty as inferior only to the blessing of a baronetcy; and the Sir Walter Elliot, who united these gifts, was the constant object of his warmest respect and devotion. (*Per,* pp. 3-4)

The prose is direct, definitive, and unambiguous to a degree that we have never before witnessed in Jane Austen. In the earlier novels, in descriptions of General Tilney, Mrs. Bennet, and Mr. Elton, the language shifts around the character; when definition occurs, it appears, as John Bayley suggests, as a form of exasperated sympathy, of humorous chastisement; it is never a substitute for personality, and further uncertainties of character are allowed and expected. Here the language closes in completely; the judgment is implacable and unchanging.

The ironic exuberance of former narrations is absent; there is no uncertainty, no sense of being occasionally surprised and generally appalled by the character. The narrator of the other novels provided these emotions and acted as an intermediary between the character and the reader's emotions about the character; the narrator's role was both to stimulate and to check these emotions. Hence the element of ironic challenge in all the novels up to *Persuasion,* an element that strongly characterizes the ironic comedies but also makes itself felt in harsher ways in the other novels. Recall one of the opening remarks of *Mansfield Park:* "But there certainly are not so many men of large fortune in the world, as there are pretty women to deserve them" (*MP,* p. 3). Like the openings of the earlier works of satiric realism, *Sense and Sensibil-*

ity and *Mansfield Park,* the opening of *Persuasion* possesses a great intensity of scorn; yet unlike the others, its assault is unrelieved by such interjections. No ironic narrator intercedes to modify or objectify the disgust. Sir Walter is viewed from the perspective of one who lives with him, whose very intimacy, like Gulliver's view of the Brobdingnagians' skin, makes derogation inevitable. The description and judgment are simultaneous, and the reader has nothing to do but accept them.

We see now that a major function of the ironic narrator was to involve the reader in the moral difficulties of the story. The above sentence from *Mansfield Park* is wholly characteristic of the crude slyness of the narrator, of her unceremonious ambition to draw the reader in by trifling with him — in this case by teasing his intelligence with a cliché. Such efforts always succeed in Jane Austen, in a way that George Eliot's narrative intrusions never can, because of their element of self-irony. There is something irresistible about irony directed against oneself; James Thurber, for example, may not be a great writer but he is an irresistible one. Jane Austen's narrator never calls on the reader with the majesty of compassion one finds in George Eliot; she never pretends to enlist the better part of ourselves. Her method is to provoke us into participation by stimulating our judgment in a variety of ways: challenging, withholding, encouraging, and satirizing it. The result is an exuberance of interchange between reader and narrator that serves to counteract the corrosiveness of many of the insights contained in the story. The absence of this exuberance is conspicuous in *Persuasion*; the narrator no longer cares what the reader thinks.

This coolness to the reader contrasts with an intensity of feeling for the characters in the story, particularly for the heroine. The reason for this contradiction is that Anne Elliot is the central intelligence of the novel. Sir Walter is seen as Anne sees him, with resigned contempt. For the first time Jane Austen gives over the narrator's authority to a character almost completely. In *Emma*, many events and situations are seen from Emma's point of view, but the central intelligence lies somewhere between the narrator and the reader, who together see that Emma sees wrongly. In *Persuasion*, Anne Elliot's feelings and evaluations correspond to those of the narrator in almost every situation, although there are several significant lapses, which I will take up later. It seems that this transfer of authority placed a strain on Jane Austen's accustomed narrative tendencies and that she could not maintain it completely.

Because Anne Elliot is fatigued and despondent, the mood of the narrative is one of resignation and exhausted care. A sense of things ended, things spent, powerfully characterizes the beginning of the novel. It appears in images of finished movement. Sir Walter slowly pages through the entire Baronetage and then closes it; his character is illuminated from "beginning" to "end"; Elizabeth Elliot cannot find a baronet "from A to Z" who suits her as much as her cousin. The exhaustion implied in these metaphors is intensified by the opening conviction that we have hit the rock bottom of moral life in Sir Walter. The often-praised mood of disappointment in the opening chapters is a result of this conviction, for the reader intuitively expects things to move upward since they cannot move downward. Yet this upward movement does not occur for some time, and so the narrative seems to become even heavier. Even the heroine participates in the oppression, because she has given up hope of influencing or changing her environment. Anne's revenge upon her father and sister is that she does not try to change them. She has been disappointed in love and is unable to get beyond the experience.

The heroine's failure to fulfill herself in the world, then, is as much a result of the feebleness of her soul as it is of the inessentiality of the world.[1] A minor dialogue later in the story seems to me to be especially illustrative of Anne's state of mind, and hence of the novel's. On the morning of Louisa Musgrove's accident, Anne and Henrietta stroll down to the sea before breakfast. Henrietta intends to marry Charles Hayter, who she hopes will become resident curate of Dr. Shirley's parish at Uppercross. They praise the morning and the breeze, then are silent until Henrietta suddenly begins:

> Oh! yes, — I am quite convinced that, with very few exceptions, the sea-air always does one good. There can be no doubt of its having been of the greatest service to Dr. Shirley,

after his illness, last spring twelvemonth. He declares himself,
that coming to Lyme for a month, did him more good than
all the medicine he took; and, that being by the sea, always
makes him feel young again. Now, I cannot help thinking it a
pity that he does not live entirely by the sea. I do think he had
better leave Uppercross entirely, and fix at Lyme.—Do not
you, Anne?—Do not you agree with me, that it is the best
thing he could do, both for himself and Mrs. Shirley? (*Per,*
p. 102)

In any of the earlier novels, the heroine's reply to such a speech
would be a difficult compromise. Like Elizabeth Bennet's words to
Mr. Collins, the response must unite civility and truth, must acknowledge the reasonable without acquiescing to the selfish. Anne
Elliot, however, senses no difficulty; to her it is a matter of "general acquiescence." "She said all that was reasonable and proper
on the business; felt the claims of Dr. Shirley to repose, as she
ought; saw how very desirable it was that he should have some
active, respectable young man, as a resident curate, and was even
courteous enough to hint at the advantage of such resident curate's being married" (*Per,* p. 102). "Very well pleased with her
companion," Henrietta chatters on until the others approach,
giving Anne only time to offer a "general answer" once again,
"and a wish that such another woman were at Uppercross, before
all subjects suddenly ceased."

Anne does not simply comply with the innocent egotism of Henrietta; she actually encourages it. It is not her courtesy but her
apathy that lends the seaside conversation its curiously soft emptiness. In *Pride and Prejudice* or *Emma* the same scene would have
been tightened with a more emphatic irony and heightened with
comedy, and therefore would have conveyed at the very least a
commitment to the character. In *Sense and Sensibility* or *Mansfield
Park* Henrietta's speech would have been treated with greater
scorn, but only in *Persuasion* could it be treated with indifference.
I am reminded of Hamlet's encounter with the court fop Osric in
the last act of the play. Earlier Osric would have aroused Hamlet's
loathing and brought on his scathing abuse; now Hamlet is mock-
ing and detached and accepts Osric out of a fundamental moral
indifference that is far more disturbing, and seems far more per-

verse, than his earlier madness. A similar atmosphere of controlled apathy, of resigned indifference, characterizes the first half of *Persuasion*. Even the unrelenting judgments of the opening page amount to a kind of indifference in their surrender to disgust. Like Anne herself, *Persuasion* walks a thin line between wisdom and apathy, between resignation and despair.

One of the remarkable aspects of the famous passage about Dick Musgrove is that it breaks through the shield of indifference into anger:

> The real circumstances of this pathetic piece of family history were, that the Musgroves had had the ill fortune of a very troublesome, hopeless son; and the good fortune to lose him before he reached his twentieth year; that he had been sent to sea, because he was stupid and unmanageable on shore; that he had been very little cared for at any time by his family, though quite as much as he deserved; seldom heard of, and scarcely at all regretted, when the intelligence of his death abroad had worked its way to Uppercross, two years before.
>
> He had, in fact, though his sisters were now doing all they could for him, by calling him "poor Richard," been nothing better than a thick-headed, unfeeling, unprofitable Dick Musgrove, who had never done any thing to entitle himself to more than the abbreviation of his name, living or dead. (*Per*, pp. 50-51)

This passage is one of the few instances in Jane Austen in which we sense a loss of control, perhaps because the exact source of the statement is confused. The sentiment of the passage comes both from a narrator (in some ways the old Jane Austen narrator appearing suddenly) and from the central consciousness of Anne. Like Sir Walter in the opening scene, Dick Musgrove is seen as the frustrated Anne might see him. He was a sailor on Captain Wentworth's vessel and enjoyed Wentworth's company when Anne was denied it. The jealous feelings that might be evoked under these circumstances would be greatly intensified by the anxiety Anne feels for rejecting Wentworth. In the judgmental description of Dick Musgrove, the intolerable blame is transferred or displaced to the foolish boy.

On the other hand, the passage contains the less neurotic, and more ironic, impulses of the standard Austen narrator. Whenever this narrator treats the subject of death, attention always focuses on how people respond to it. In *Persuasion*, the question of one's response to loss is of particular interest; many of the characters are widows, and the heroine herself is figuratively widowed. Austen's contempt for the Musgroves' self-serving grief, and for their coarse foolishness in choosing to like their son *after* he is dead, is consistent with her treatment of human evasions in general, and of the persuasions and evasions of *Persuasion* in particular.[2]

Yet Austen's attitude toward evasion does not explain the extraordinary vehemence of the passage and the hatred of the dead boy that is revealed in it. The statement is aberrant and uncontrolled; it suggests, perhaps above all, the pathology of disillusion. The novel of disillusion is always in danger of losing its irony and of simply demanding meaning in outright form. I have discussed the opening despair of *Persuasion*, which is felt in the debilitating emotions of the heroine herself. The Dick Musgrove passage reads like a terrible and irrational outburst against this despair: an exasperated attempt to force meaning—even negative meaning—onto the despondent world. In the insincerity of their grief, the Musgroves exemplify the Sartrean condition of "nothingness": like the French waiter who plays the role of the French waiter, the Musgroves play the role of grieving parents. For the first time in Jane Austen the narrative irony cannot sustain the insincerity, and in a burst of frustration the narrator makes some claim for the diabolical truth.

The animus behind the statement ("and the good fortune to lose him") is as anarchic as a modern conception of truth usually is. The narrator is saying that some lives really are worthless. This is the dark, unfamiliar side of the narrator's characteristically didactic insistence that some lives really are worth something.

The judgment on life is not confined to the Musgroves and their dead son but is applied even to the heroine herself. It is often said that Anne, unlike previous heroines, has nothing to learn. But unsettling suggestions in the narrative imply that the author felt Anne has much to learn. Her friendship with Mrs. Smith constitutes an education, particularly with regard to the information about Mr. Elliot's character. On her walk to Mrs. Smith's the morning after the concert at which Wentworth has betrayed his jealousy of Mr. Elliot, Anne thinks about Mr. Elliot's suit and magnanimously regrets that she will have to discourage him: "There was much to regret. How she might have felt, had there been no Captain Wentworth in the case, was not worth enquiry; for there was a Captain Wentworth: and be the conclusion of the present suspense good or bad, her affection would be his for ever. Their union, she believed, could not divide her more from other men, than their final separation" (*Per,* p. 192). Had the passage ended here, we would not question her sentiment, but it is followed by a harrowing interjection: "Prettier musings of high-wrought love and eternal constancy, could never have passed along the streets of Bath, than Anne was sporting with from Camden-place to Westgate-buildings. It was almost enough to spread purification and perfume all the way" (*Per,* p. 192). The variety of interpretation of this passage indicates how individual each reader's understanding of Austen's tone can be. Marvin Mudrick, in general so stringent an interpreter of Austen's irony, sees this passage as a sincere "burst of affection" from Jane Austen herself. "We share the author's overt sympathy," he writes, in an instance of "unalloyed joy."[3] I confess to bafflement at such an interpretation. The passage seems to me directly and passionately hostile in its irony; nothing could be more antithetical to Austen's conception of love than the image of purification and perfume. The statement is another example of the sudden, uncontrolled outburst of the authorial mind. As in the Dick Musgrove passage, the hostility is pathological but understandable. Anne is on her way to visit Mrs. Smith, who has no suitors to choose from, no money, and few friends. It seems a grotesque luxury for Anne to insist that, given her choice of suitors, she would only choose Wentworth and love him eternally. The passage is an angry defense of those who have to make do with what they have.

Jane Austen wrote *Persuasion* during her illness under circumstances similar to those of Mrs. Smith. In a curious way, she seems to blame Anne for feeling the isolation and sadness that Mrs. Smith would be justified in feeling. A poverty-stricken invalid possesses a cheerful fortitude, while Anne Elliot indulges in tender sonnets of declining happiness and, unlike the farmer, does not mean "to have spring again."

During the visit with Mrs. Smith Anne learns of Mr. Elliot's true character and of instances of inhumanity that make Sir Walter seem harmless. The confrontation of her own worldly ignorance makes her humble; and, at the close of the chapter, her assurance of the invulnerability of her love for Wentworth has disappeared: "Anne could just acknowledge within herself such a possibility of having been induced to marry him, as made her shudder at the idea of the misery which must have followed. It was just possible that she might have been persuaded by Lady Russell!" (*Per,* p. 211). If this humility survived to an admission that she was wrong to take Lady Russell's advice in the first place, *Persuasion* would be a novel of education, like the ironic comedies. But Anne eventually decides that she was right, and her refusal to learn from her mistake is one reason why *Persuasion* is not a novel of education but one of disillusion—the characteristic nineteenth-century form. Anne Elliot has something to learn but does not quite learn it. As in her insistence on unrequited constancy to Wentworth, it is as if Anne must have everything, must be right even in the past. She never confronts the issue of persuasion, as Wentworth confronts his own stubbornness. (He admits he stayed away too long out of angry pride.) Anne's main failing is that she is too "tender," as the closing lines suggest, too excessively "feminine." Wentworth admits his stubbornness, and he even mocks the masculine pieties when he says, " 'I have been used to the gratification of believing myself to earn every blessing that I enjoyed. I have valued myself on honourable toils and just rewards. Like other great men under reverses,' he added with a smile, 'I must endeavor to subdue my mind to my fortune. I must learn to brook being happier than I deserve' " (*Per,* p. 247). In *Persuasion,* the feminine pieties are never mocked, although they are occasionally undermined. Anne's maternal longings and her desire to be needed, for example, make her grateful when people are hurt or unwell and she can care for them. But because Anne herself is the central consciousness of the novel, the author's reservations about her disposition or preferences remain ambiguous and faint.

Either because of Austen's inexperience in working within a central consciousness or because of her inability to revise the novel completely before her death, the transference of perception is never fully controlled. Despite occasional judgments against her, too much power is given to Anne Elliot—too much power, one may say, over the other characters in the story. In one respect, Louisa Musgrove's accident is an act of revenge, a symbolic murder of Anne's rival. And the story becomes the imaginative fulfillment of Anne's fantasies. Had Jane Austen lived to write more novels, she would have mastered the technique (had she chosen to) and been able to center her intelligence inside a character without either violating the actuality of circumstance or destroying the moral realism that the old narrator had so responsibly maintained. Or, as for example in *Middlemarch* or *Washington Square*, she would have perceived and exploited the connection between fantasy and circumstance, and shown the mind's ability to impose its fantasies on the world.[4] The fact that Jane Austen was making these changes in narrative method, however, and that, for example, *Persuasion* strongly influenced *Washington Square*, justifies Leavis's placing Austen at the head of his tradition. Austen attempts to transfer the narrator's authority to the isolated consciousness of Anne Elliot in order to conform to a new conception of society and of the individual's place in that society. The changes in English society that were to separate the world of *Emma* from that of *Portrait of a Lady* were well underway at the end of Austen's life, and she recorded them in *Persuasion*.

Persuasion is the first novel by Jane Austen, for example, in which society is conceived of no longer as a meaningful whole, but as a series of disparate parts. Both *Mansfield Park* and *Emma* rely on an ethos of place for their sense of society; the organized propriety of Mansfield and the cooperative energy of Highbury provide each novel, and the characters in them, with a clear sense of context. But *Persuasion* is made up of a meaningless variety of places and the conflicting minor identities that attend them: Sir Walter's Kellynch Hall, Uppercross Cottage, Uppercross Great House, the Hayters' farm, the Crofts' Kellynch Hall, the various habitations of Lyme and Bath, and so on. It is perhaps for this reason that in *Persuasion* social structures are contemplated with almost systematic dissatisfaction. The society of *Mansfield Park* is an infected whole, but a whole nonetheless; its only virtue lies in its ability to provide some context for the individual. In *Persuasion* this last consolation has disappeared. The heroine moves from place to place, disoriented, isolated. Almost every community and form within which she functions is made meaningless by sheer disparity, or by the inevitable necessity of removal.

For this reason, Anne Elliot may be said to be "alienated" — certainly the first heroine in Jane Austen to be so, and perhaps the first in English fiction. She passes beyond the mere loneliness of Fanny Price and the magisterial conceit of Emma, into an egocentric isolation very similar to that experienced by Dorothea Brooke or Isabel Archer. For Anne is genuinely estranged — overcome and enfeebled by her homeless condition. Her fate will never flow into the communities through which she passes, and her marriage signifies a movement out of the communities she has known. The navy represents the only adequate community in the novel, and Anne's final association with it provides the only antidote to what would otherwise be a completely private resolution or an exclusively lyrical finish. But the special status accorded to the navy is qualified by its precarious military destiny, as the last page of the novel suggests.

The robust security of *Emma,* written a few years before *Persuasion,* comes precisely from this safety from alienation, from its implicit confidence that a reconciliation between interiority and reality, between Emma and Highbury, is possible. The same may be said of *Mansfield Park*, whose reconciliation is actually enhanced by its joylessness. Its population purged and reshuffled, Mansfield finally opens itself to meaning, and the piteous integrity of Fanny Price is at last rewarded. Fanny had always struggled to maintain the connection between interiority and reality. (Compared to her, the Crawfords seem "free," as indeed they are, because they have released themselves from the struggle.) Self-deceiving as she sometimes is, only Fanny probes continually: how much of what I feel or know to be true can I perform? For both Fanny Price and Emma Woodhouse the way is open to salvation, and through various comic and tragic struggles and sacrifices, salvation is attained: the embracing of an outside order that corresponds to interiority, and that therefore includes love. For the modern soul who seeks fulfillment in this correspondence with reality, as Lukács has said, irony must be the texture and form of his experience, but this irony does not compromise the ideal itself, which is the lived experience of meaning in the world. When the ideal is attained, as it is at the close of all Jane Austen's novels except the last, it is experienced to some degree by more than just the main characters; it is, or was, potentially accessible to all.

This belief in the possiblility of common meaning and common destiny is greatly weakened in *Persuasion*. Unlike the conclusions of the earlier novels, that of *Persuasion* does not resound with other marriages, but rather with a series of failed unions. We do not feel that others will follow Anne into paradise. Even the marriage between hero and heroine has far less communal significance than those of earlier novels, for the navy is an accidental home for Anne, as Kellynch Hall is for the Crofts. The sense of impermanence felt in *Persuasion* anticipates the anxieties of many nineteenth-century novels.

The moral and aesthetic order sustained by Austen's earlier narrators, then, is no longer possible in the dislocated world of *Persuasion*. As a result, Anne Elliot — whose social circumstances make her a passive observer — almost becomes the central consciousness of the novel. Yet the transference of moral perception is never complete, because Anne is still too dependent on the various communities she visits. She can judge the Musgrove girls, for example, but not completely or absolutely (the way the authorial voice judges Mrs. Bennet in the first chapter of *Pride and Prejudice*); Anne lives among the Musgroves and knows she lives among them. She is in a position to resist them in certain ways but not to decide against them. She is more isolated than the earlier heroines but still she must participate; she does not have the choices, say, of Jane Eyre, Dorothea Brooke, or Isabel Archer.

The opening portrait of Sir Walter is perhaps the best example of what Austen could do within the new mode of perception produced by the loss of a narrative frame. Sir Walter is inelastic, implacable, conceptualized. There is no air between him and the author's conception of him. He is a fixed image in the book, and Austen's genius makes him so. In *Emma* Austen explored questions of human nature in a Shakespearean way; in *Persuasion* her sense of the social world she wrote about had changed so as to make this approach impossible. The description of Sir Walter paging through the Baronetage in search of his own name and lineage, or contemplating his reflection in his mirror-filled room, is a psychological portrait of the dissociation of the self. Sir Walter is a man in search of an existence, in search of some exterior proof of his existence in the world. He derives his existence from the volume, and he bestows in it the existences of others. Birth, death, and "heir presumptive" are recorded there. One of the novel's closing ironies is Wentworth's acquisition of an existence in Sir Walter's eyes: Sir Walter inscribes his name in the Baronetage.

The portrayal of Sir Walter is a social portrait of the dislocation of role. Role is the self's "job," the self's direction, and Sir Walter fails in his role as the baronet of an estate. *Persuasion* deals with the crisis of separation between self and role in society. In an increasingly democratic society, such separations are inevitable as individuals assume roles they were not born to (the Crofts move into Kellynch) and lose roles they were born to (Sir Walter is forced to leave). The basic uncertainties in the novel separate it markedly from Austen's earlier works.

Persusasion is the only one of the novels that ends with a vague ignorance of where the hero and heroine are going to live, and even of what the years will bring for them. Wentworth does not have an estate, and the novel's close acknowledges the possibility of another separation to come (another war). The nature of society in *Persuasion* makes assurance about the future impossible, and therefore causes a loss of personal assurance. (Uncertainty about the future is what leads Anne to reject Wentworth in the first place.) Unlike the earlier heroines and their lovers, Anne and Wentworth, or the love between them, lack the simplicity of will to overcome illusions and obstacles; they fail before the novel opens. Nowhere is Austen's irony more emphatic than in the beginning of her dénouement: "Who can be in doubt of what follows? When any two young people take it into their heads to marry, they are pretty sure by perseverance to carry their point" (*Per,* p. 248).

Let us now take a closer look at the social world of *Persuasion.* Actually the term "social world" is slightly misleading. We can speak of the social world of *Pride and Prejudice,* of the Mansfield estate, of Highbury, but the world of *Persuasion* is made up of separate and divided communities of opinion and idea, of imagination and memory: "Anne had not wanted this visit to Uppercross, to learn that a removal from one set of people to another, though at a distance of only three miles, will often include a total change of conversation, opinion and idea" (*Per,* p. 42). From Uppercross she moves to Kellynch-Lodge, Lady Russell's house: "When they came to converse, she was soon sensible of some mental change. The subjects of which her heart had been full on leaving Kellynch, and which she had felt slighted, and been compelled to smother among the Musgroves, were now become but of secondary interest. She had lately lost sight even of her father and sister and Bath. Their concerns had been sunk under those of Uppercross" (*Per,* p. 124). And from Kellynch-Lodge she moves to her family's house at Bath: "Uppercross excited no interest, Kellynch very little, it was all Bath" (*Per,* p. 137). The only continuity among these worlds is Anne's consciousness: "It was highly incumbent on her to clothe her imagination, her memory, and all her ideas in as much of Uppercross as possible" (*Per,* p. 43). Only Anne is aware of the mental distance among the different locales she inhabits. This awareness above all sets Anne apart from the closed consciousnesses of other persons.

In the first part of *Persuasion,* until Anne's arrival at Bath, the separation of mind is primarily perceived as a separation of place. As Anne visits one house after another, she encounters different states of mind: Kellynch-Hall, Uppercross cottage and Uppercross Great House, Lyme, Kellynch-Lodge, and Kellynch-Hall again with the Crofts inhabiting it. At Bath all worlds seem to converge: the Crofts, Elliots, Musgroves, and Harvilles, and Lady Russell, Anne, and Wentworth all join there, and two figures out of the past, Mrs. Smith and Mr. Elliot, appear to make the convergence total. Yet the convergence is deceptive, and the geographical unity only serves to set off the actual disunity of the society. Distinctions of estate now become distinctions of street, as Sir Walter keeps reminding us. And the closer social milieu of Bath only seems to emphasize class distinctions in the minds of the people who live there. Elizabeth Elliot's unexpected invitation to Wentworth only confirms our consciousness of her conceit, for she is convinced that he will be flattered and grateful to receive it, just as she and her father are grateful to receive an invitation from the Dalrymples. Class snobbery is always criticized in Jane Austen, yet only in *Persuasion* is it presented with unrelieved seriousness and simplified disapproval. The Price family's relative poverty in *Mansfield Park* was clearly linked to their insensitivity. In *Persuasion*, Mrs. Smith's poverty is more genteel that the Elliots' wealth; the snobbery that ostracizes her is a destructive illusion. Similarly, Lady Dalrymple and her daughter, latter versions of Lady Catherine de Bourgh and her daughter, have an emptiness that is too offensive to Jane Austen to tempt her to treat them humorously, to allow them any eccentricity that could redeem their self-important mediocrity.

The sense of individuality gathers intensity throughout the novel, until at Bath all the characters are like so many autonomous beings, encountering one another with haphazard regularity, each expecting and seeing something unique to his or her self, each oblivious of the others. The reconciliation of Anne and Wentworth takes place gradually through a series of accidental encounters; that the proposal itself is spurred by an overheard conversation and realized in a note increases our sense of the tenuousness of human interchange. Even characters who pride themselves on their shrewd awareness, like Mr. Elliot in his understanding of Mrs. Clay, are always blind at some crucial point. Preoccupied with Mrs. Clay's ambitions with Sir Walter, Mr. Elliot overlooks her ambitions with himself. These disparities of view and personality are seen to originate in the disparities of age, experience, physical appearance, and family with which the novel is preoccupied. The narrative is saturated with allusions to differences between persons: Lady Russell's manners are old-fashioned and Elizabeth Elliot's are not; those who are in the navy see things differently from those who are not (even down to the painting of the ship that irritates Admiral Croft); those who are young and attractive are different from those who are not; Mrs. Musgrove is fat and Anne, we are told several times, is slender. These details give *Persuasion* a dimension that is not felt in the other novels. *Pride and Prejudice*, for example, underplays all differences but those of mind; it opens with the disembodied voices of the Bennets. Physical differences, class differences, and so on are realized only in differences of state of mind. The same is true, though to a lesser degree, of *Emma*, in which communal interaction encompasses individual difference. In *Persuasion*, the individual is at once independent and estranged, looming and yet powerless.

The confidence of *Emma* in a stable, cooperative community is lost in the social and personal fragmentation of *Persuasion*. As a result, the heroine is far more uncertain. The ever changing egotism of the environment is too much for Anne to resist; hence her compliance with whatever environment or situation she is in. This compliance ranges from apathy (with Henrietta) to sympathy (with Benwick) to resignation (with her family) — all passive responses.

In discussing *Emma* I stressed the importance of the idea of cooperation in Jane Austen, and I pointed out that Austen saw a distinction between cooperation and compromise, restraint and repression, that we no longer see. This changes in *Persuasion*. Social cooperation assumes a stable community in which individual cooperation ultimately benefits the individual: Emma and Highbury go together. *Persuasion* does not have a Highbury at its base, a communal form with its own memory and imagination in which an Emma could participate and thrive. Its heroine is the more uncertain Anne Elliot, who moves from community to community, and who can only comply rather than cooperate. She is happy to be "of use," which is to say that in the different environments she enters, she is being used. The personal damage such a posture incurs is fully realized later in the century by Henry James in the character of Madame Merle. Madame Merle is another woman whose life is a series of visits to other people's houses, and who by necessity cultivates an ability to comply while preserving a secret will. Anne Elliot's secret intelligence is far from the indomitable and uncooperative will of Madame Merle, yet she too must live with secret consolations: "Anne always contemplated [the Musgrove sisters] as some of the happiest creatures of her acquaintance; but still, saved as we all are by some comfortable feeling of superiority from wishing for the possibility of exchange, she would not have given up her own more elegant and cultivated mind for all their enjoyments" (*Per,* p. 41). In statements like these Anne Elliot reminds us of many nineteenth-century heroines. We think of her in these instances almost as a "case": an unmarried, unoccupied women, superior in mind and character to all about her, yet unrecognized, unnoticed, and even shunned among them. In a reversal of the case of Emma Woodhouse, Anne's situation defines her more than her personality does. And that, of course, is her problem, and the problem of so many other Victorian heroines.

Anne's consolation represents the Victorian (and modern) variation of stoicism. It is not the consolation we are asked to accept in *King Lear*: that Cordelia's goodness is its own reward. Anne's protective conviction of her own rare "cultivated mind" seems to state that the burden of intelligence is its own reward: that the estranged consciousness is better than the communal stupidity. This awareness of the enforced isolation of the sensitive and thinking person appears in the complaints of Victorian intellectuals. John Henry Newman, who admired Jane Austen's novels, complained that the age was becoming "the paradise of little men, and the purgatory of great ones," and Matthew Arnold complained in a letter to A. H. Clough that the society was becoming "more comfortable for the mass, and more uncomfortable for those of any natural gift or distinction." Although both had in mind the decline in "great careers" of men, their sentiment is fundamentally analogous to Austen's intuition of the burden that both the mediocrity and the discontinuity of social life place on the intelligent and sensitive person.

This resentment of social life takes us back to the first half of *Sense and Sensibility,* to Marianne's Blakean exasperation with the insincerity of society. In the earlier novel, however, the burden is ultimately shown to have its source in the illiberal illusions of its sufferer, for several of the seemingly unfeeling supporters of society (from Mrs. Jennings to Elinor) turn out to be sincere, while the romantic lover is actually shallow and worldly. In *Persuasion* suffering is also rooted in a particular weakness of the heroine, yet social life remains intolerable to the end. In its general structure, *Persuasion* registers a fundamental, almost Weberian crisis of belief in the legitimacy of social structures. Certainly one of the most radical statements in all of Jane Austen is Anne's subversive sentiment concerning her father's departure from Kellynch-Hall; that "they were gone who deserved not to stay, and that Kellynch-Hall had passed into better hands than its owners" (*Per,* p. 125). As Weber has said, established power is sustained only through a subjective belief in its legitimacy, through people believing it is legitimate and allowing themselves to be so dominated. Revolutions begin with a crisis of legitimacy. In *Persuasion* we see the beginning of a failure to support traditions, a failure that led to nineteenth-century reforms. The positive feeling toward the navy lies in its widespread invigoration of domestic life. In the words of Sir Walter, the navy was "the means of bringing persons of obscure birth into undue distinction, and raising men to honours which their fathers and grandfathers never dreamt of" (*Per,* p. 19). As the closing lines of the novel suggest, Austen rated the domestic advantages of this revitalization as equal to the military achievements of the navy. "Anne gloried in being a sailor's wife, but she must pay the tax of quick alarm for belonging to that profession which is, if possible, more distinguished in its domestic virtues than in its national importance" (*Per,* p. 252).

These alterations in social life are perceived as transformations within and among families. As always in Jane Austen, the basic instrument of both division and unity is the family, of which marriage is the origin. Class feeling is an extension of family feeling, or pride of ancestry, as the opening of the novel makes clear. Jane Austen originally entitled her work *The Elliots*; her brother Henry changed it after her death to perhaps the more ingenious title. Yet the first title may hint at what Austen meant to explore: a family's mind and future. The culmination of Sir Walter's ancestral account is "Heir presumptive, William Walter Elliot, Esq., great grandson of the second Sir Walter" (*Per,* p. 4). The question of inheritance is central to many English novels and crucial to those of Jane Austen. Because she centered on the destinies of women, this question has been overlooked, together with her concern for establishing the difference between legal and rightful, between material and moral, inheritance. In their concern with the passage of generations, all the Austen novels pose the question that Lionel Trilling perceives in Forster's *Howard' End:* "Who shall inherit England?"[5] In the opening pages we learn that William Elliot is the heir presumptive, but Mr. Elliot's part in the plot is relatively insignificant; like all the novels, *Persuasion* focuses on the actual inheritors. Anne and Wentworth inherit the England of *Persuasion,* if only because they see it, and will experience it, as it really is: fragmented and uncertain. For the first time in Jane Austen, the future is not linked with the land, and the social order is completely dissociated from the moral order. William Elliot will inherit the improverished Kellynch, but that does not matter. The future is in the hands of Anne and Wentworth, as the present is in the hands of the Crofts, that almost comic national couple whose defense of England abroad makes them the rightful inhabiters of Kellynch. It is significant that to Anne the only temptation to marry Mr. Elliot is that she would inherit her mother's position at Kellynch. Her rejection of him makes clear a distinction between familial and moral inheritance.

Anne's marriage to Wentworth represents an act of will to replace, through marriage, the old inadequate family with the new adequate family, an act that is at the core of the generational concept of every Jane Austen novel. The feminine conception of marriage, unlike the masculine one, traditionally assumes loss as well as gain, because until well into the nineteenth century only the woman left her family when she married; the woman also, of course, lost her name and assumed a new one. A basic movement in all Jane Austen's mature novels is the heroine's struggle to create a new "family" for herself, to replace with a new relationship the unsatisfactory family in which she is unappreciated or unfulfilled. In *Persuasion* the sense of the pains of the original family is particularly keen. Sir Walter and Elizabeth's most serious failing is their lack of feeling for Anne. And Lady Russell's concern to see Anne married is analogous, in its awareness of the need for escape, to the concern felt for all the heroines after *Sense and Sensibility*. "[Lady Russell] would have rejoiced to see her at twenty-two, so respectably removed from the partialities and injustice of her father's house [through marriage to Charles Musgrove]" (*Per*, p. 29).

In Jane Austen marriage represents a reorganization of social life. Anne sees her marriage in part as the formation of a new social group, and regrets that in that respect she can offer so little: "[Anne] had no other alloy to the happiness of her prospects, than what arose from the consciousness of having no relations to bestow on him which a man of sense could value. — There she felt her own inferiority keenly" (*Per*, p. 251). The marriage that ends *Persuasion* is viewed as part of the general revitalizing of English society that took place upon the navy's return from the war.

The revitalizing power of marriage is suggested in all the Austen novels, but most urgently, most despairingly, in *Persuasion*. In the earlier novels, marriage is linked to the general functioning of the society and to the land; marriage is a form of participation in society. In *Persuasion*, society no longer offers the couple a defined context for their adult identities; compared to Elizabeth and Darcy, Anne and Wentworth are directionless after their marriage. For this reason, the individuals themselves and the relationship they embark on carry a great burden. Marriage is no longer sustained by a larger framework; Anne Elliot will not receive the spontaneous social support and identity that Marianne Dashwood receives when, upon her marriage to Colonel Brandon, she finds herself "placed in a new home, a wife, the mistress of a family, and the patroness of a village" (*SS*, p. 379). Mary Musgrove "would not change situations with Anne," for "Anne had no Uppercross Hall before her, no landed estate, no headship of a family" (*Per*, p. 250). Whatever social strength Anne and Wentworth's marriage possesses will be created and sustained by themselves. For this reason, the singular existence and quality of the marriage itself becomes vitally important.

It is the individual's lonely responsibility for his entire future that perhaps gives *Persuasion* its powerfully ambiguous mood. The closing marriages of the earlier novels seem to represent pos- siblility more than necessity, a stage in the moral growth of the heroine, the nexus of generational change. In *Persuasion*, mar- riage between Anne and Wentworth is a matter of sheer need, the last hope for the individuals themselves and for the dissolving so- ciety around them. In the closing felicities of *Emma,* as I have said, we understand the different marriages through comparison. This statement holds true with a vengeance in *Persuasion.* Most of the major characters are literally or figuratively widowed; and among the complete pairs, only Admiral and Mrs. Croft possess a moral existence. The only hope of the novel rests almost entirely upon two characters, Anne and Wentworth, who are alike in their superiority of mind and sensibility and yet are alienated from each other.

For this reason, the progress of Anne and Wentworth's recon- ciliation is fraught with tension and significance. All the novels are imbued with a tension between the pains of the present and the hopes of the future; and all implicitly contrast the lovers with the lesser world around them. The emotional intensity of *Persuasion* is heightened by the addition of another dimension: the past. Together with a sense of the isolation of the heroine, the use of the past is responsible for the intensity of feeling contained in the reconciliation of Anne and Wentworth.

Like *David Copperfield, Persuasion* poses the question: is the past a pain or a pleasure?[6] The pains of the present are rooted in Anne's past mistake, but so are the hopes for the future. The past seems to envelop the whole; we feel the hero and heroine are mov- ing forward and backward in time simultaneously. This paradox lends the novel an urgency that is at once painful and hopeful. The exquisiteness of the novel's emotion, like that of Shelley's poem to the West Wind, lies in the consciousness that spring will come. Also as in the poem, this consciousness is held in check; it is realized only momentarily in Anne's feelings of fearful happiness. The dominant experience of the novel is one of loss; the move- ment, though urgent, is downward.

The mood and feelings imparted in the beginning of *Persua-*

sion—the sense of resignation and regret, the feeling of the inalterable circularity of time expressed in the seasonal imagery, and the inescapable redundancy of life expressed in allusions to the eventless years preceding the opening of the novel—gather intensity when Anne learns of Wentworth's return. Then very gradually Anne's despair is replaced by a desire to act; like the farmer plowing the field, Anne finally "means to have Spring again." As this feeling grows, the sense of time lost and wasted becomes more intense. The hope for spring only makes the winter more acute.

Even though we know that Anne and Wentworth will be reconciled (either from previous reading or from romantic expectation) the novel seems to swirl downward to this conclusion. In the compression of events at Bath, there is a sense of rushing toward the reconciliation as though it were a last chance, as indeed it is. The grace of the language gives the novel an eerie quality because it contrasts so sharply with the separateness of events, the dislocation of characters. This grace may be why the novel is so frequently called "elegiac"; it possesses the grace of despair, the grace of giving way to despair.

Perhaps because of this weight of despair, *Persuasion* is Jane Austen's finest expression of her view of time and personality as ambiguous movement, as continual reorganization that has both progressive and regressive tendencies. There are no apocalyptic endings in Jane Austen; there is never a revolution, only a regeneration of attitudes. The heroine is never completely enlightened—that is to say, she is never as enlightened as the author or as the reader potentially is about her situation. Anne Elliot cannot take the final step in self-awareness by admitting that she was weak to take Lady Russell's advice, the step that would make the close of the novel a totally new beginning. Complete transcendence is not to be expected. That Anne and Wentworth are reconciled must satisfy us. In Jane Austen, social and personal changes are never absolute. That Austen could not conceive of a total revolution of consciousness is apparent in one of the most interesting minor incidents in all of her novels, Anne's response to Mr. Elliot's insulting letter about her father. He calls Sir Walter a fool, which Anne and the reader and the narrator know him to be. The issue at hand is one of filial respect, but still Anne's response intrigues us: "Anne could not immediately get over the shock and mortification of finding such words applied to her father" (*Per*, p. 204). The significance of Anne's indignation is that it shows us she has some family feeling after all; and who among us has not experienced the same thing, the same surprise of feeling an involuntary allegiance toward those one has ceased to care for? Anne cannot be fully conscious of her past any more than she can transcend all ties to her family or to Lady Russell. Personal and social change in Jane Austen comes about through the ceaseless reorganization of persons through marriage; in the words of her contemporary Erasmus Darwin, it consists of the power of "delivering down those improvements by generation to its posterity, world without end!"[7] In her earlier novels, Jane Austen showed that right marriages are socially and morally vital to the worlds in which they are realized. In the environment of *Persuasion*, in which the individual's social identity is in a state of collapse, the marriage of "intelligent love" becomes, for the well-being of the individuals involved, a stark necessity. And when we consider the peculiar, intense concern and suppressed hope with which later novelists were to invest the marriages of their heroes and heroines — the marriages, for example, of David Copperfield, Dorothea Brooke, and Isabel Archer — we see that the ambiguous, autumnal mood of *Persuasion* comes from neither sentimentality nor sickness nor oncoming death, but from a full consciousness of the fate of marriage in the century to come.

7

Jane Austen
as a Woman Writer

History books often tend to assume that until women began to demand a political existence they had no existence at all. This assumption suggests the political bias of historical theory in general —its preference for the "heroic" and its neglect of the domestic. Some contemporary histories indicate a change of sensibility in their attention to the immediate social existence of a particular era; and although Jane Austen's novels correspond well to the new, more integrated histories, few studies have undertaken to explore the connection. The novels are commonly, and often unconsciously, viewed in relation to the official history of markets and empires. Seen in this light (or shadow), the novels must yield to one of two judgments: either they are elegantly, perhaps unforgivably, evasive, or they are subtly, perhaps ingeniously, microcosmic. Criticism based on the latter, less predictable view often tends to pass over Austen's central concerns altogether and concentrate on what the novels imply about masculine destiny or the political destiny of the society. Of the essays that view her subject more directly, few are without some momentary assertion of puzzled amazement—amazement over her ability to make so *much* over so *little!*[1] Little concerns in fact imply feminine concerns, or the concerns of ordinary life.

An example of "microcosmic" interpretation is V. S. Pritchett's description of Jane Austen as a war novelist. He points out that the facts of the long war are basic to her books. She knew all about the shortage of men, about the high cost of living, most particularly about the vital part played by the navy. This approach is highly perceptive and diverting, and Pritchett is of course being deliberately outlandish with the term "war novelist." Yet the same has not been said of Thackeray, even half-humorously; as the battle of Waterloo is tangentially perceived in *Vanity Fair*, there is no need to justify Thackeray's seriousness. And this is what Pritchett attempts to do; he is saying, "You see, she really was aware of the important things after all." The fact is that in *Persuasion* Austen was interested not in the war itself, but in how people got together afterward, in what finally the war was for. She was interested in how civilized existence replenishes and stabilizes itself, not in how it is torn apart. Her deference to local, civilized history constitutes a conception of history, not an evasion of it.

In our discussion of Jane Austen as a woman writer, the question of war is emblematic and interesting. We recall the classic criticism, that she neglects the Napoleonic wars. Few critics today accept that as derogation, but only because they have found other, and more subtle, political significance in the novels, such as class conflict. The complaint that Austen did not write about the Napoleonic wars has one source in classic literary-historical standards of subject matter. Greatness of style, Ruskin contended in *Modern Painters,* requires the choice of noble subject, by which he meant war, religion, and passion (widespread historical interests, profound passions, sacred subjects). The second level of subject matter is the portrayal of great men in history, and the third the representation of ordinary life. Here we see one of the basic differences between traditional masculine and feminine cultural attitudes. War is historically not a noble subject to women. Until this century, the feminine half of the population did not participate in war except through the intensification of its ordinary pursuits, such as nursing. And while democratic conscription of men is a relatively modern phenomenon, participation in war has always signified a possibility in the minds of men: the opportunity to become hero or coward in the face of death. It does not represent the same possibility to women, not even the possibility of dying, except passively, through invasion. Because war has not wrenched women from their communities and placed them in a separate community, and often in a foreign country, to fight, war has not changed women as immediately as it has changed men. And although women incur loss in times of war, they also incur loss in times of peace. War is a horrifying time for women, as Homer well knew in his portrayal of Andromache. They have nothing to gain and everything to lose. And while it is not necessarily ignoble, war is no more a "noble" subject to women than gambling is to men. In fact, had she chosen to examine it in itself, Jane Austen might have viewed war the way Pushkin views gambling in "The Queen of Spades": as revealing a desperation that is both symptom and cause. The indirect view of war in *Persuasion* is decidedly satirical; the navy men long for another war to make money, and Captain Wentworth goes on enthusiastically about his war profiteering. The novel closes with the wry observation that the navy is "if possible, more distinguished in its domestic virtues than in its national importance." Such a statement is consistent with a feminine viewpoint. The critical discomfort with Austen's definition of war as a domestic experience more than a political one is part of a more ancient masculine discomfort with this preference in the feminine outlook.

Even though the novel genre is antiheroic by definition, the classical literary-historical standards of subject matter have survived in attitudes toward it. This survival is shown in one of the most persuasive essays written on Jane Austen in recent years, Graham Hough's study of *Emma*. The novel, he writes, "has entered into an engagement with history," an engagement that Austen fulfills as an English novelist but not as a world novelist. In the long perspective of class history that Hough has adopted, Austen's novels are "strongly ideological constructions" and "powerful reinforcements of a particular class structure and of a moral structure adapted to support it."[2] As the class whose ethos she is enforcing was to be culturally dominant throughout the nineteenth century in England, Austen is deservedly considered a great English novelist. But no more than that, according to Hough, because she accepts the values of the English upper bourgeoisie as nonhistorical absolutes. She deliberately refuses to attend to the leakage of consciousness from one class to another that always exists in bourgeois society.

One cannot argue with Hough's conclusions; given his historical assumptions, they are impeccable. But it is questionable whether this perspective is, in the final analysis, a fruitful approach to fiction, or even an accurate approach to Jane Austen. When Hough writes, "Charlotte Corday, Mary Shelley and Bettina von Arnim were among her contemporaries . . . but Jane Austen returns us to the ethos of the Rambler," his deference to the radical minority is disturbing.[3] Jane Austen was the contemporary of women like Charlotte Lucas, Mary Bennet, Maria Bertram, Emma Woodhouse, and Anne Elliot. Are we to assume that Jane Austen and the anonymous women she wrote about are not history, and that Mary Shelley and the Frankenstein monster are history? In her attention to the anonymous sex, and in her articulation of the femimine ethos, Jane Austen was as revolutionary in her own way as Mary Wollstonecraft.

Hough understandably views the history of Jane Austen's day as revolutionary history. He writes, "The world of which her novels present a corner was a world in convulsion, filled with wars, revolutions, the struggle for political liberty, black repression, miserable poverty and savage penal laws."[4] It was also a world in which communities continued to cohere and flourish in spite of these happenings, and in spite of their knowledge of them. Jane Austen's novels are not unconscious of the miseries of her day; as B. C. Southam has shown, she treats them "by silent implication." One of her major achievements, he writes, "is to have captured the total illusion of the gentry's vision, the experience of living in privileged isolation."[5] In *Pride and Prejudice,* Catherine and Lydia bring home the gossip: "Much had been done, and much had been said in the regiment since the preceding Wednesday; several of the officers dined lately with their uncle, a private had been flogged, and it had actually been hinted that Colonel Forster was going to be married" (*PP,* p. 60). What is being shown here, for those who care to notice, is more effective than any direct description of a flogging could be: the monotony, calmness, and acceptability of cruelty, the way it fits unobtrusively into our world. We may have more to learn about how violence continues in society from Jane Austen than is generally supposed. It is not surprising, at any rate, that those writers who have undertaken to observe violence directly, like Melville and Lawrence, have also been capable of arguing its political necessity.

Before we can consign Austen's novels to a "corner" of the world, then, we must understand better the connection between political change and domestic stasis, between political violence and domestic nonviolence, between the world in convulsion and the supposed ongoing peace of domesticity. *Mansfield Park, Vanity Fair*, and *War and Peace* are similar in the way they liken military to domestic experience. The Mansfield estate is itself like a warship, run by an irresponsible lieutenant, Mrs. Norris, while the captain is away. In *Persuasion*, the war is seen to have a more paradoxical effect upon society; it offers men of ability, like Captain Wentworth, the opportunity to make money and therefore to rise in society.

Erik Erikson suggests that feminine history, or domestic history, balances the official history of territories and domains; that marriage and family life maintain the stability and continuity of civilization, which political and economic divisions and crises tend to corrode. Overlooking Mary Beard's history, he claims that the unofficial history has yet to be written of women's creativity "in preserving and restoring what official history had torn apart."[6] In a curious way, Jane Austen's view of the world was the reverse of Tolstoy's opening perception of *Anna Karenina:* to Jane Austen, corrosion is uniform, repetitive, and therefore not a rich subject for fiction; while vitality and organization are unique, problematic, and infinitely discoverable.

Jane Austen's novels convey an idea of everyday existence centered around the experiences of marriage and family life. That Hough views everyday existence as a corner of the world reveals his inheritance of classical standards of subject matter. Yet part of the greatness of Austen's novels, as of many modern novels, lies in their unrelenting insistence that everyday existence is *not* a corner of the world. It is frequently remarked that more than almost any other novelist Jane Austen can be read and reread with increasing delight. This quality comes from the sentence-to-sentence brilliance of the novels, which speak of the moment-to-moment brilliance, the transitory meaning, of the everyday life she describes.

A cardinal attribute of the novel genre is the acknowledgment of ordinary life. Except in the novel, and occasionally in satire and comic drama, the conventional everyday life of unexceptional persons is unrepresented in literature. In this fidelity to everyday, unheroic existence, the novel as genre has always had a special relationship to women's history. From its inception women have made up the major audience and often the major subject of the novel. Austen drew on Richardson as she did on Fanny Burney in her delineation of a feminine consciousness.

What is a feminine consciousness? Recent studies of minority history have shown that even the most oppressed class is not utterly dehumanized by the experience of oppression, but develops its own traditions, values, and compensations. The compensations are familiar to any reader who has noticed the role of the servant in the English novel; but the values and strengths, or the active consciousness, of a politically suppressed group are somewhat more elusive.

The existence of a feminine consciousness is suggested in Jane Austen's first five novels. Although her women lead restricted lives, her novels are not about restriction, nor even about expression, but about the relationship between the two, about how women find ways to develop and assert their womanhood despite the restrictions placed on them. Though there are women in the novels who fail to do so—who, like Charlotte Lucas, settle for demoralizing compensations—the heroine always succeeds. The world in which we find her at the close of the novel is as much molded by her as she has been molded by the world.

In the educated class of Austen's society, the influence of women was especially powerful. Because their oppression did not extend to the experiences of poverty and illiteracy, educated women were more equipped to counter their political unimportance. They were also the members of a class that had reached a point never reached before in the cultivation of arts and letters. Many great and small houses of the gentry made art, science, and polite letters as central to rural society as sport, agriculture, and politics. And for the first time among gentlemen a regularized standard of manner and speech was observed. According to G. M. Trevelyan, "The country houses and the world of fashion did more for culture and intellect at that time than the dormant universities."[7] As eighteenth-century fiction testifies, women were as actively present in this society as men. And Austen seemed to be aware that women in her own class received better treatment than in any below it. When Fanny Price returns home to visit her poor and striving lower-middle-class relations, her family hardly notices her. All attention and praise go to her brother, whose career in the navy is the focus of the family's hopes.

It is not surprising, then, that the class and atmosphere of the gentry produced the first major woman author in England, a novelist who undertook not only to reveal the influence and importance of women in her class, but to articulate the unspoken-for values of her sex. "Men have had every advantage of us in telling their own story," says Anne Elliot. "I will not allow books to prove any thing." Jane Austen herself well knew that novels do not endeavor to prove the little claims and opinions of mankind, but that they do testify to something larger, the energies of culture and spirit. The feminine consciousness may be seen as one such unacknowledged energy. For until the feminist movement began to succeed, feminine history was, by and large, a great anonymous tradition, a set of values and beliefs that were passed on through generations of women, from older to younger women, from mothers to daughters. Following certain crude models in earlier fiction by women, Austen's novels were the first to voice this consciousness.

The feminine ethos of Austen's novels is primarily located in her view of social life. Briefly, this view is characterized by a generational definition of moral life, a concern for the actual and immediate quality of social existence, a belief in human interdependence, and a value for social cooperation and personal adaptability. These preferences make up the feminine consciousness of Austen's first five novels, or the discrete consciousness of educated women until the impact of the Industrial Revolution.

The feminine consciousness was a mode of perception, a kind of social conscience, developed both by Austen's culture and by the women in her culture for the sake of collective survival as well as individual security and fulfillment. Culminating at the end of the eighteenth century, this consciousness began to disintegrate and change soon after; *Persuasion* is the first novel in which the value and importance of being a woman in her society is held in question. By Charlotte Brontë's time, the feminine confidence in social cooperation and personal adaptability had all but disappeared; cooperation had become submission, adaptability had become subservience. In Austen's first five novels, cooperation and humiliation have nothing to do with one another, for the uncooperative self is often the debased self.

Let us consider the feminine consciousness in detail. In the first component—a generational definition of moral life—the word "generation" suggests the idea of evolution or biology. Yet the nature of the feminine consciousness as it is expressed in Austen's novels is distinctly intellectual rather than biological. The generational structure of her fiction is above all a moral structure. This is why so little significance is attached to motherhood as a biological function, why motherhood is established by character and feeling rather than by blood. Hence the multiplicity of surrogate parents in Austen's fiction. Mothers who are involved in their children as children, as mere objects of affection and entertainment rather than educable beings, are always deficient mothers. Nor is it necessary for the heroine, the enlightened woman, to bear children in order to have a moral destiny. As Elizabeth Bennet influences Georgiana Darcy or even as Emma influences Harriet, the older influence the younger, the stronger influence the weaker.

The generational structure of Austen's novels has already been discussed at length. All the novels explore the connections between generations, the mistakes of the past and the hopes of the future. At the center of generational change stands that archetypal figure, the uncommitted young woman. The strength of generations depends on the process by which she and the man she chooses find their respective identities, fuse them in love and marriage, revitalize their traditions, and together bring up the next generation, just as Elizabeth and Darcy are to bring up Georgiana at the end of *Pride and Prejudice*. In marriage, whatever dispositions have developed earlier in life become permanent. The moral characters of Charlotte Lucas and Lydia Bennet seem to freeze in time after their marriage choices, because they have become part of the whole process of production and procreation that marks adulthood.

The relations between older and younger women are central to the generational structure of Austen's fiction, for the influence that passes between generations is of vital significance to the moral education of the young. Mrs. Gardiner takes an interest in Elizabeth Bennet's growth, and Elizabeth values this interest. In *Persuasion*, the pivotal relationship exists between Anne Elliot and Lady Russell, not between Anne and Captain Wentworth. Edmund Wilson was puzzled by this; he wrote of Lady Russell's importance to Anne as a deficiency in the novel, evidence perhaps of the author's failure to mature.[8] He overlooked Lady Russell's function as a role model, to use the contemporary term. Several times in the novel, Lady Russell's importance to Anne as surrogate mother, as moral guide, is stressed. Wilson's essay is, incidentally, a classic of sexist literary criticism. Classic because of its fineness of insight, yet mercilessly biased, from the condescending familiarity of its title, "A Long Talk about Jane Austen" (Who would entitle an essay, "A Long Talk about Herman Melville"?), through the suggestion that the two female scholars whose work he discusses have subjectively identified with the heroines, to his puzzled disapproval of Emma's "infatuation with other women." Marvin Mudrick follows up the last point by saying, as though it were something shocking, "The fact is that Emma prefers the company of women," and that this "tendency is certainly never made explicit."[9] In many novels with male protagonists, the hero's relationship with other boys or men is an obvious and instrumental element in his growth. The pivotal relationships in *David Copperfield* are not between David and Dora or David and Agnes, but David and Murdstone and David and Steerforth. In Jane Austen, the heroine is always a woman who likes other woman; this is evidence of her basic health, her natural identification with those of her own sex as a means of self-awareness and growth. By contrast, women who are completely male-directed, and there are many in Jane Austen, are either fools or deceivers who are themselves deceived.

The generational structure of Austen's novels indicates a conception of time and history that is regenerative. As in *Emma*, this sensibility is antiteleological; it views time and experience as a regenerative continuum. It is continual versus final, regenerative versus apocalyptic. Enlightenments in Jane Austen are never absolute; in *Emma* they are repetitive. Austen's social history is a perpetual reorganization of relationships through marriage. It is regenerative in the sense that change renews, by forever producing new combinations of experience.

Many of Dickens's novels center on the change of generations yet in their latent structure are apocalyptic. *Dombey and Son*, like the train that is its central image, rushes toward a particular destination. The family picture that dominates the close of the novel shows us the final family, not the family as part of a continuum. The characters have learned everything they are going to learn, and the story finishes with a satisfying flourish. Austen's view of family survival is far more impersonal and uncertain—a movement from marriage to marriage, contingent on other persons, and therefore full of change and mystery. The charm of Austen's endings is that they are unsettling; most of the characters who had something to learn, from Emma to Mrs. Elton, have not quite learned it. Mrs. Elton is Mrs. Elton to the last line of the novel, and Emma's future with Mr. Knightley will not always, we feel, possess the perfect meeting of minds that their wedding briefly symbolizes. The open-ended structure, the view of experience as continuum, is of course far more prominent in later novelists, like Woolf, Proust, and Joyce.

The splendid consequence of this wise and undemanding view of the future is a highly demanding view of the present, an unrelenting concern for the actual and concrete condition of personal and social existence. Arnold Kettle pinpoints this sensibility very nicely when he writes of *Emma*: "Hartfield is offered to us as Hartfield, not as Life . . . And this ultimately, I think, is the strength of *Emma*: this rejection of life in favor of living, the actual and concrete problems of behavior and sensibility in an actual, concrete society . . . It is this concern that gives her such delicate and precise insight into the problems of personal relationships (how will a group of individuals living together best get on, best find happiness?")[10] Curiously, even this valuable praise of Austen misrepresents her perceptions. For it is not how a group of individuals living together "best" get on, "best" find happiness, but simply how they function at all, given their actual, not their ideal, propensities. For like Darcy, Austen's characters often display a discrepancy between their theoretical and actual behavior.

Behind the concept of getting on is the simple, staggering realization that we must all get on together, that we are interdependent beings. Jane Austen's novels unabashedly assume human interdependence. The belief in independence that plays such a significant part in the masculine consciousness, and hence in our tragic literature, does not occupy a place in her novels. She omits it not simply because the women in her society were forced by laws and customs to be dependent, but because she saw human interdependence as a universal condition. Before *Persuasion*, she viewed limitations on women's lives ironically, but not exactly negatively—although she undoubtedly owed some part of her unique, ironic style to the pressure of oppression. The lack of movement, the limited number of new acquaintances, the dominance of family, the unavoidability of neighbors, the need for escape through marriage, were all recognized as difficulties rather than as oppressions. Elizabeth Bennet is first seen trimming a hat, curious about the arrival of an eligible bachelor in the neighborhood. Emma has never seen the seaside and does not care to. The destinies of Marianne Dashwood and Fanny Price, which we may consider dismal, are nevertheless sanctioned by the whole social ethos of each novel.

As a result, the novels before *Persuasion* place a high value on cooperation and adaptability as social acts that do not entail a compromise of integrity. Austen consistently draws a distinction between cooperative integrity (Elinor Dashwood) and calculating conciliation (Lucy Steele). D. W. Harding's description of Jane Austen's society applies with complete truth only to *Persuasion*: "In such a society there are degrees of isolation. A high degree is created by the civil falsehood and polite evasion ('Emma denied none of it aloud and agreed to none of it in private') which break true social contact and leave the speaker in a position of tacit superiority but cut off from his hearers."[11] Harding describes the restraints required by society as producing "social detachment." I have tried to show in the chapter on *Emma* that, according to Austen, such restraint produces the opposite effect. "Civil falsehood" and "polite evasion" are derogatory terms for courtesy; courtesy in Jane Austen (especially before *Persuasion*) is a form of cooperation and harmony, and a means of social engagement. At Box Hill, the civility and politeness Harding describes are momentarily put aside by Emma, and we see the result, hardly an example of "true social contact": Miss Bates is placed in a condition of social estrangement. In these novels, the defiantly "honest" act is often the defiantly petty act or even the defiantly cruel act; and persons who pride themselves on their honesty—Marianne and Mr. Palmer in *Sense and Sensibility*, for example—are actually priding themselves on feelings of superiority. Mr. Palmer is never guilty of the civil, false, and polite evasion Harding decries: "He entered the room with a look of self-consequence, slightly bowed to the ladies, without speaking a word, and, after briefly surveying them and their apartments, took up the newspaper from the table and continued to read it as long as he staid" (*SS*, p. 106). Later, Elinor interprets his behavior: "It was rather a wish of distinction she believed, which produced his contemptuous treatment of everybody, and his general abuse of everything before him. It was a desire of appearing superior to other people. The motive was too common to be wondered at" (*SS*, p. 112).

The distinction between truth and falsehood is ambiguous in Jane Austen, as it is in any mature writer. Certainly a major question in *Sense and Sensibility* is the connection between "verbal" truth and other kinds of truth. How much is a verbal truth or falsehood worth in comparison to the truth or falsehood of a situation? "Marianne was silent; it was impossible for her to say what she did not feel, however trivial the occasion; and upon Elinor therefore the whole task of telling lies when politeness required it, always fell" (*SS*, p. 122). Marianne is a moral child, who sees only one kind of truth in all situations; this trait becomes her greatest punishment, for she attaches herself to someone with the same limited conception of honesty. Like Marianne, but unlike her in knowing exactly how far he can go, Willoughby never commits a *verbal* falsehood in engaging Marianne's affection. It is Elinor who perceives the larger truth of a given situation, or the necessity for an attitude of cooperative tolerance in social life.

Before *Persuasion*, the adjustments people make to preserve social harmony are not failures but successes of the spirit. Darcy is better for having to know and appreciate the Gardiners. Jane Austen draws a distinction between adjustment and concession that Harding does not recognize. Charlotte Lucas's marriage to Mr. Collins is a concession to worldly values; it is in no sense an adjustment of the self. If anything, it reveals a complete inflexibility of the spirit. As Elizabeth sees when she visits her, Charlotte gives nothing of herself to her husband; she sits in the room she knows he will avoid and ignores him generally. "When Mr. Collins could be forgotten, there was really an air of comfort throughout, and by Charlotte's evident enjoyment of it, Elizabeth supposed he must often be forgotten" (*PP*, p. 157). Austen perceives marriage as a cooperative endeavor, and as a morally uplifting experience because it is cooperative. All the novels affirm the function and potential of marriage to "improve" the individuals involved. Generally, the self that refuses to accommodate to others, particularly to those closest, is the degraded self; the self that succeeds in accomodating (Darcy) is spiritually expanded. The merging of classes in *Pride and Prejudice* is an extension of the cooperative instinct in individuals to marry in spite of class differences.

Much is absent from this consciousness, just as much is absent from feminine history in general; its achievement and fulfillment are collective—not always, and not necessarily, individual. The few women who did seek autonomous identities, like the political minority Graham Hough mentions, were not Jane Austen's concern; her interests were more radical than the liberal imagination of our own age is likely to conceive. She wished to discover where the unacknowledged energy of so many educated women, women like Elizabeth Bennet and Emma Woodhouse, was finding expression. And she found it to be hidden in life itself. Echoing Oscar Wilde, we could say of almost every heroine, of Emma above all, that she gave her *genius* to her life. And like Wilde's, each woman's life loses something in the selectivity of creation.

Jane Austen was fully aware of the price that women paid for joining in the particular, selective consciousness of femininity; just as she knew the unutterable vacancy of feminine life without that consciousness. Of Mrs. Bennet's existence she gives a simple, devastating summary: "The business of her life was to get her daughters married; its solace was visiting and news." Only the comedic brilliance of *Pride and Prejudice* and the knowledge that Elizabeth's "business" and "solace" will be finer than her mother's can mitigate the Sartrean "nothingness" expressed in that sentence.

Ironically, the feminine consciousness that I have identified received its finest expression at a moment in history when social changes were beginning to make it obsolete. It is an indication of Jane Austen's artistic integrity that she acknowledged these changes in her last novel. *Persuasion* is the only Austen novel in which social cooperation and personal adaptability are more than problematic virtues, in which they are potentially dangerous poses to adopt — above all, dangerous for women to adopt. Anne Elliot is too gentle and persuadable, traits that are perceived as part of her femininity. Dutiful and compliant, she allows herself to be persuaded to give up the man she loves. For the first time in Jane Austen, Victorian sexual identities are strong enough to create the novel's central dilemma.

The social world of *Persuasion* is ripe for feminism. The long war had polarized the sexes psychologically, and in *Persuasion* we see the new respect for "masculinity" that attended the polarization. Wentworth is the most virile of all the Austen heroes; and Sir Walter Elliot comes under criticism largely because he is a feminized male, with his mirror-filled room, his "Gowland," and his excessive concern with the facial complexions of others. Even the curious, uncontrolled denunciation of Dick Musgrove, who had been a midshipman on Captain Wentworth's vessel, may be explained in part by an awareness that it was out of *this* material that "strong" men like Wentworth and Admiral Croft fashioned the means to defeat Napoleon. And Charles Musgrove's judgment of Benwick reflects the respect for physical prowess that comes with war: "I have a great value for Benwick; and when one can but get him to talk, he has plenty to say. His reading has done him no harm, for he has fought as well as read. He is a brave fellow. I got more acquainted with him last Monday than ever I did before. We had a famous set-to at rat-hunting all the morning, in my father's great barns; and he played his part so well, that I have liked him the better ever since" (*Per*, p. 219). It is difficult to imagine this mode of judgment in the context of *Pride and Prejudice*; Mr. Bennet takes Darcy hunting, but praises him for his conversation.

It follows that the heroine of the environment of *Persuasion* has difficulties relating to the new polarity of the sexes; we see in Anne herself the sentimentalization of femininity that exists in wartime societies. Anne is more classically feminine than any other Jane Austen heroine; it is even in observing her powers of "healing" that the soldier, Captain Wentworth, renews his love for her. Tender, cooperative, sensitive, delicate, maternal, sympathetic, she is at last too feminine, too "tender", as the closing lines of the novel forbode. Jane Austen never subscribed to the tiresome prescription that sexual identities complement one another, like fish and chips; and it is clear from *Persuasion* that she found the sexual stereotypes of postwar England divisive and burdensome. In each of the novels the similarities, intellectual and moral, between hero and heroine are greater than the differences; and the search for a spouse is a search for someone of equal intelligence and sensitivity in a world of cruder minds. One feels that each hero and heroine could say to one another what Arnold once said in a letter to Clough: "with all our differences we agree more with one another than with the rest of the world."[12] Until *Persuasion,* the differences arise haphazardly from temperament: Elizabeth is aggressive, Darcy is shy, Jane Fairfax is serious, Frank Churchill is gay. But in Jane Austen's last novel these invigorating disparities have disappeared, and the contrast between hero and heroine has taken on all the dull, uninventive tones of convention: Captain Wentworth is strong, Anne is weak, he is defiant, she is dependent, he is tough, she is tender. The real test for both Anne Elliot and Captain Wentworth, and for the love between them, is to penetrate

the lifeless barrier composed of these clichés. In their final reconciliation, Victorian sex roles are reversed: the woman speaks, and
the man relents.

Yet the level of enlightenment contained in their reconciliation
is different for each and, in the case of the heroine, riddled with
irony. It can be argued that Wentworth is preparing for his realization all along; even his provoking assertion that women should
not be allowed to travel on navy vessels is a disguised criticism of
Anne's fragility. Later, he faces up to the illusion of his own masculine "independence" when he admits to staying away too long.
Anne's psychological progress is painful and ironic by comparison.
Unlike Wentworth, she has not enjoyed even the illusion of independence, and the feminine virtues of passivity and "feeling" have
completely debilitated her. After eight years of loveless estrangement, she is no longer able to "make Spring come." And when it is
time to interpret the crucial decision of her past, the closest she
comes to self-knowledge is a recognition of her own right, as a
woman, to choose the more protected path. The whole question of
feminine consciousness in this novel seems finally to revolve
around those intensely felt debates over what women can *endure*,
what they should be asked to endure, and what kinds of strength
are available to them as beings who have been *made* dependent.
Only until Anne herself speaks out on the subject does her silent
suffering seem broken at last: "All the privilege I claim for my own
sex (it is not a very enviable one, you need not covet it) is that of
loving longest, when existence or when hope is gone" (*Per*, p.
235). This statement perhaps contains more self-criticism, and
more regret, than is generally recognized.

Of all the novels, *Persuasion* is the most conscious of the deficiencies of feminine life, deficiencies both internal and external.
Together with the inner weakness imposed on and expected of
women, Anne Elliot suffers from the external failures of her class.
Persuasion records the financial and social impoverishment of the
gentry at the beginning of the nineteenth century. In the opening
chapters, we are given a sense of the vacancy of domestic life for a
woman of this class. Anne Elliot has nothing to do; as an
unmarried woman and younger daughter, she has no active func-

tion in either family or community. Making a farewell visit to the tenants of Kellynch is her only communal responsibility in the entire novel; and after her family leaves the estate, she has no role but that of babysitter or nurse. As shown earlier, Austen's last novel contains for the first time in her writing the suggestion of an irrevocable breach between interiority and society. Anne Elliot is alienated; she has no place, no function, and, until she marries, no active social identity. Even as Wentworth's wife, her identity and future are more uncertain than those of any earlier heroine. In place of an estate, Captain Wentworth offers her only the naval community; and, as the closing lines of the novel suggest, this community must live in expectation of disruption.

Historical circumstances favored the earlier heroines. Women belonging to the landed gentry of the late eighteenth century were nearly equal to their husbands in responsibility. In rural families the husband and wife lived and worked together in almost uninterrupted association from season to season, year to year. Each had serious duties connected with the economy of household and field; and when the man was away for home guard or wartime obligations, the woman was responsible for keeping the family going by managing its lands and household economy. Mary Beard writes that not until "the commercial and political revolutions, accumulating full force in the eighteenth century, actually disrupted the solidarity of . . . families founded on a landed wealth did women alike with the great families to which they belonged lose most of their power which they had so long exercised."[13] Not until then, she argues, did the state pass to the control of parliaments composed by men and elected by men. It was a loss of power, then, as well as a desire for it, that gave rise to feminism among educated women.

Household economy was of course a much larger responsibility in a nonindustrial society than it is today. The mistress of an estate, large or small, had extensive and serious responsibilities. (In Elizabeth's phrase, to be mistress of Pemberley really *would* be something.) A mother was above all responsible for managing the education of her children, particularly her daughters; and idle or amoral mothers in Jane Austen have a devastating effect on their daughters—Mrs. Bennet on Lydia, Lady Bertram and Mrs. Norris on the Bertram girls. Parents who, like Lady Middleton, perceive and love their children as finished rather than educable beings, are always inferior parents.

As Mary Beard has shown, the lives of men and women in rural families were equal and integrated. Elizabeth and Darcy, Emma and Knightley will spend a great deal of their time together because their responsibilities are home-centered. To understand the effect that professions would have upon women of this class who were, for example, moved to the cities, we have only to compare Isabel Knightley's married life with what we know Emma's will be like. Isabel is married to a London lawyer who divides his time between work and family and has little energy for anything else. She spends all her time at home with her children and the doctor, Mr. Wingfield. Although these are latent suggestions, it is significant that John Knightley views his family as both the pleasure *and* the burden of his life; this suggests, I believe, the modern male-professional view of the family—an ambivalent one. As women have fewer and fewer responsibilities, they become greater and greater burdens to their working husbands. The burden of the wife is a topic of conversation in *Persuasion*—what does one do with Navy wives?

In rural families the husband and wife viewed the home as their joint territory. Yet when the man's profession began to take him away from home, the home became the almost exclusive territory of the woman. This territorial division between men and women has continued to the present day; it is revealed, for example, in Thurber's famous cartoon of the husband coming home from work to a house in the shape of a woman. The separation of husband and home and the decline of feminine responsibility contributed to the polarization of sex roles that characterized the Victorian age. As a reading of Shakespeare or Fielding reveals, this polarization had not been a major characteristic of sexual identities before then.

The sexual stereotypes that arose from this separation are bourgeois. They began to take their peculiarly overpowering form in Samuel Richardson's first novel, *Pamela*, which originated as a model of letter-writing etiquette for young women who wished to adopt middle-class manners. In Walter Scott, the Victorians found two of their basic stereotypes, the frivolous girl and the mysterious, passionate woman, as John Henry Raleigh has shown.[14] By 1850 with the publication of *David Copperfield* and, a few years earlier, *Vanity Fair*, the stereotypes had become fully accepted and were therefore under examination in fiction. In Victorian fiction we encounter repeatedly the frivolous and pure "girl" figure (Scott's Rose Bradwardine and Thackeray's Amelia Sedley), the mysterious, passionate woman (Scott's Flora MacIvor and later, Dickens's Edith Dombey), the morbid and religious child-adolescent (Dickens's Little Nell; Twain's Emmeline Grangerford), and the pragmatic "Aunt Polly" adult woman (Twain's Aunt Polly and Dickens's Aunt Betsey Trotwood). Masculine stereotypes always accompany these types: the frivolous girl-figure requires a responsible husband-father; and Aunt Betsey has her Mr. Dick. It is the nature of sexual myth that it is attended by resentment. If the stereotype is unveiled, as Amelia Sedley begins to be revealed as a "tender little parasite," the character begins to be despised.

Many explanations have been offered for the polarization of the sexes that is revealed in these types: the formulation of a middle-class family ethic, the rise of evangelicalism. Certainly the girl-figures originate partly in the ethic of purity that Walter Houghton analyzes in his chapter on love and sex in *The Victorian Frame of Mind*.[15] I have suggested that the increase in professions caused a literal division of the sexes on a large scale. Sexual stereotypes are part of the sexual mythology of the middle class, and they have survived with certain alterations today.

Jane Austen is conspicuously free of the sexual stereotypes and character conventions one finds in so many nineteenth-century novels. John Bayley is correct in classing Jane Austen with Shakespeare and Tolstoy in her ability to create characters in "the irresponsible plastic way". Austen's personalities, like those in Shakespeare, elude sexual identity. In *Emma*, for example, as Mary Ellmann points out, "[the] contrast between Emma and Knightley is as much in age as in sex, so that vivacity seems to belong as much to youth as to femininity . . . And before them both, to stimulate indulgence of each other, there is Mr. Woodhouse. Feminine caprice and masculine sense yield simply to time: in both sexes, vivacity is succeeded by judgment, and judgment by senility."[16] Yet Austen's freedom from the stereotypes has as much to do with the era and class in which she grew up as it does with her greatness as a writer, for she began writing before the stereotypes had firmly taken hold. Freedom from sexual stereotyping is part of a larger freedom from sexual resentment. Austen views the essentially masculine pursuits—the preoccupation with guns and dogs, for example—with amused indifference. Men who are wrapped up in sport in her novels, like Sir Thomas Middleton and Charles Musgrove, are like children, foolish but not harmful. Of course the women of Jane Austen's class rode in the hunt as well as the men. Because the women of the gentry had roles and responsibilities of their own, they were not as concerned with the real or imagined differences between male and female.

Except in *Persuasion* Austen is unlike later women writers in her indifference to the occupations that generally excluded women, for Jane Austen was confident of the opportunities of feminine expression to a degree that was impossible for Charlotte Brontë or George Eliot. As Mary Beard's description of rural life suggests, the commercial and political changes that were fully realized in the nineteenth century changed the life and status of educated women for the worse. Only in Austen's last novel do sexual identities become sexual polarities and therefore major obstacles to personal happiness. *Persuasion* is at heart a feminist novel, the prototypical novel of feminist "feeling"—an unpolemical examination of the restrictions, the crippled inner life and the monotonous outer life, of feminine existence. It marks the beginning of a tradition in literature that includes Charlotte Brontë, George Eliot, and Virginia Woolf—all very different writers but all joined in their critical concern with the nature and meaning of feminine life.

NOTES
INDEX

Notes

1. An Introduction to the Novels

1. This lack of receptivity may be seen in the critical preoccupation with what the novels exclude, as a basis for analysis and judgment, rather than what they include. A traditional assumption seems to be that Jane Austen restricted her subject matter to "3 or 4 Families in a Country Village" out of necessity (she was inexperienced in other matters) or convenience (she took the material at hand because, as a satirical observer of mankind, any social setting would do) and that this restriction, if it does not exempt her from the ranks of great novelists, at least casts doubt on the quality of her imagination. Her famous deprecators, Mark Twain and Charlotte Brontë, grounded their disgust on the limitation of character and environment. And the opinions of admirers often retain the same assumption. The approbation of readers from Walter Scott to George Henry Lewes came from an enthusiasm for Jane Austen's scrupulous fidelity to ordinary life, an enthusiasm that was modified only by a recognition of her subject's limits. "Her circle may be restricted," wrote Lewes, "but it is complete. Her world is a perfect orb, and vital." In the present century, appreciation is less qualified and at the same time more condescending toward the actual subject matter of the novels. The approach is analytical; attention is no longer focused on the commonplace social experience of the novels, except insofar as it may be seen as a microcosm of some larger moral universe. Both attitudes are fundamentally preoccupied with what is *not* present in the novels. Although in the minds of Jane Austen's nineteenth-century readers this preoccupation could not impinge on the excellence of what remained, the assumption is everywhere lurking that her achievement in the small pond compensates for her failure in the open sea. Twentieth-century critics, on the other hand, have made the restriction of subject matter into a virtue: a source of irony and a basis for objectivity. Only rarely is the idea entertained that Jane Austen chose to write about customary experiences because she found them interesting or important in themselves.

2. Ian Watt, ed., *Jane Austen: Twentieth Century Views* (Englewood Cliffs, N.J.: Prentice-Hall, 1963), p. 2.

3. Sigmund Freud, "Reflections upon War and Death," trans. E. Colburn Mayne, in *Character and Culture,* ed. Philip Rieff (New York: Collier Books, 1963), pp. 123-124.

4. None of Jane Austen's predecessors disciplined himself so fiercely to accept the boundaries of common life as the boundaries of his imagination. As E. Rubenstein suggests, "Fielding tended always toward epic, even in a 'domestic' novel like *Amelia;* while Defoe's predilection for the extraordinary and the criminal, Richardson's for intrigue and violence, and Sterne's for wildly eccentric behavior, all left the field of the ostensibly commonplace open for Jane Austen." E. Rubenstein, ed., *Twentieth Century Interpretations of Pride and Prejudice* (Englewood Cliffs, N.J.: Prentice-Hall, 1969), p. 10. Although Maria Edgeworth and Fanny Burney anticipated Austen in some respects, their pictures of ordinary social life lack the resonance found in Jane Austen, perhaps because they were not convinced of the significance of such ordinary life. In *Evelina,* Evelina has nothing to learn at the beginning of the novel except how not to offend people; and her marriage to Lord Orville is not given the emblematic weight of a marriage in Jane Austen.

5. Quoted in Lionel Trilling, *The Liberal Imagination* (Garden City, N.Y.: Doubleday, 1950), p. 205.

6. Ibid., p. 209.

7. E. M. Forster, *Aspects of the Novel* (New York: Harcourt, Brace, 1927), p. 75.

8. Jane Austen, *Emma,* p. 7. This and all subsequent references are to the editions of R. W. Chapman. Abbreviations are as follows: *Northanger Abbey (NA), Sense and Sensibility (SS), Pride and Prejudice (PP), Mansfield Park (MP), Emma (E), Persuasion (Per).*

9. John Bayley, "The 'Irresponsibility' of Jane Austen," in *Critical Essays on Jane Austen,* ed. B. C. Southam (London: Routledge and Kegan Paul, 1968).

10. Q. D. Leavis, Introduction to *Mansfield Park* (London: Macdonald, 1957), pp. xiv-xv.

11. See D. W. Harding, "Regulated Hatred: An Aspect of the Work of Jane Austen," in Watt, ed., *Jane Austen: Twentieth Century Views,* pp. 166-179.

12. Dorothy Van Ghent, *The English Novel: Form and Function* (New York: Harper and Row, 1953), p. 101.

13. Rubenstein, ed., *Twentieth Century Interpretations of Pride and Prejudice,* p. 8.

14. It is surprising how frequently the issue of the author's unmarried status comes up in essays about her novels. Since we have almost no information pertaining to the significant personal events of her life, such conjecture cannot help us understand the novels and can only reveal, as it usually does, the curiosity or bias of a particular critic toward unmarried women, particularly unmarried women writers. E. Rubenstein's comments are not unusual: "On February 20, 1817, Jane Austen was already poor in health, in fact within six months of death. But even had her physical condition been better, she could not reasonably have looked forward to a life of anything but incurable spinsterhood, for she was a pretty hopeless forty-one years old. Thus marriage could no longer have claimed the immediate personal concern it doubtless had when she began writing fiction, and biographical considerations once again fail to explain the artist's choice of subject. Yet, a mature woman in mature control of a unique talent, she still centered her work upon the activities of young women faced with the exigencies of finding and marrying the right man." Rubenstein, *Twentieth Century Interpretations of Pride and Prejudice,* p. 9. The implication seems to be that the author's choice of subject relates entirely to her personal aspirations; and that, in failing to get a husband herself, she should have turned to another subject in her fiction. But the real giveaway comes later. I wonder if we would ever speak of Melville as a "mature man"?

15. Brian Southam, *Jane Austen* (London: Longman Group, 1975), p. 45.

16. Mary Lascelles, *Jane Austen and Her Art* (London: Oxford University Press, 1939), pp. 41-83.

17. Van Ghent, *The English Novel,* p. 101.

18. A. Walton Litz, *Jane Austen: A Study of Her Artistic Development* (New York: Oxford University Press, 1965), p. 24. For a brief discussion of the matter, see R. W. Chapman's *Facts and Problems* (Oxford: Clarendon Press, 1948), pp. 149-150.

19. See Christopher Clay, "Marriage, Inheritance, and the Rise of Large Estates in England, 1660-1815," *Economic History Review,* 2d ser. 21 (1968): 503-518. According to Clay, "Marriage and inheritance can explain the rise of individual families at all levels of landed society, and at most periods in English history." His article explains "the prominence of marriage and inheritance in the rise of so many land-owning families" in Jane Austen's period.

20. Lawrence Stone, *The Crisis of the Aristocracy,* abridged ed. (London: Oxford University Press, 1967), p. 23.

21. Ibid.

22. See Stone's discussion of marriage, ibid., pp. 269-302.

23. See Christopher Lasch, "The Suppression of Clandestine Marriage in England: The Marriage Act of 1753," *Salmagundi* 26 (Spring 1974): 90-109.

24. Miriam J. Benkovitz, "Some Observations on Woman's Concept of Self in the Eighteenth Century," in *Women in the Eighteenth Century and Other Essays,* ed. Paul Fritz and Richard Morton (Toronto: Samuel Stevens Hakkert, 1976), p. 40.

25. Two recent studies, however, have made Austen's conservatism their subject: Alistair M. Duckworth's *The Improvement of the Estate: A Study of Jane Austen's Novels* (Baltimore and London: Johns Hopkins Press, 1971) and Marilyn Butler's *Jane Austen and the War of Ideas* (Oxford: Clarendon Press, 1975).

26. Laurence Lerner, *The Truthtellers: Jane Austen, George Eliot, D. H. Lawrence* (New York: Schocken Books, 1967), p. 150.

27. See Lerner's discussion of this passage, ibid., p. 152.

28. Loren Eiseley, *Darwin's Century* (Garden City, N.Y.: Doubleday, 1961), p. 348.

29. Ibid., p. 344.

30. Tony Tanner, Introduction to *Sense and Sensibility* (Baltimore: Penguin, 1969), p. 9.

31. See the discussion of *Pride and Prejudice* in Litz, *Jane Austen,* pp. 84-112.

32. My chapter on *Persuasion* (chapter 6) focuses on how and why Austen's use of an authorial voice diminished in her last novel. Anne Elliot almost becomes the central consciousness of the novel because she is a passive observer; and because the moral and aesthetic order sustained by former Austen narrators is no longer possible in the dislocated world of *Persuasion.*

33. Lionel Trilling, ed., *The Experience of Literature, Fiction* (New York: Holt, Rinehart and Winston, 1967), p. 101.

34. R. W. Chapman, ed., *Jane Austen's Letters,* 2d ed. (London: Oxford University Press, 1932), p. 286.

35. See essays on Jane Austen by Lewis and Schorer in Watt, ed., *Jane Austen: Twentieth Century Views.* In this chapter, and more extensively in the chapter on *Emma,* I take up the matter of Austen's Johnsonian strain. The accounting metaphors that Mark Schorer has insisted are central to Jane Austen's view of social life had ceased to be metaphors by the time they reached Jane Austen; they had been totally assimilated into the language for at least a century, and had appeared in Fielding

and Dr. Johnson as unselfconsciously as they appear in Jane Austen. They show that England is a commercial nation but not that its writers have an acutely commercial sensibility. They stand out in Jane Austen only because her prose is without metaphor. They would not look like metaphors if she had consciously used metaphors in the context that surrounds them.

36. Graham Hough, "Narrative and Dialogue in Jane Austen's *Emma*," *Critical Quarterly* 11-12 (1967): 201-229.

37. Ibid.

38. Lascelles, *Jane Austen and Her Art*, p. 102.

39. Bayley, "The 'Irresponsibility' of Jane Austen," pp. 1-2.

40. Northrop Frye, *Anatomy of Criticism* (Princeton, N.J.: Princeton University Press, 1957), p. 226.

41. Michael Wood, "Heroine Addiction," *The New York Review of Books* 23, no. 5 (April 1, 1976):13.

2. The Two Prototypes: *Northanger Abbey* and *Sense and Sensibility*

1. Q. D. Leavis, "A Critical Theory of Jane Austen's Writings," *Scrutiny* 10 (1941-1943):61-87, 114-142, 272-294; 11 (1944):104-119.

2. The apologetic "Advertisement by the Authoress" to *Northanger Abbey* reveals Austen's awareness that the novel relied strongly on that particular audience.

3. Tanner, Introduction to *Sense and Sensibility*, p. 15. Foucault is quoted by Tanner.

4. Ibid., p. 20.

5. Lionel Trilling, *Beyond Culture* (New York: Viking, 1968), p. 38.

6. John Fowles, *The French Lieutenant's Woman* (New York: Signet, 1969), p. 102.

7. Tanner, Introduction to *Sense and Sensibility*, p. 28.

8. Ibid., p. 30.

3. Necessary Conjunctions: *Pride and Prejudice*

1. Henry James, *Partial Portraits* (New York, 1888), pp. 391-392.

2. Time in *Pride and Prejudice* calls to mind Wittgenstein's definition of eternity: "If we take eternity to mean not infinite temporal duration but timelessness, then eternal life belongs to those who live in the present." (*Tractatus Logico-Philosophicus*)

4. The Victorian Anxieties of *Mansfield Park*

1. Virginia Woolf, "Jane Austen" in Watt, ed., *Jane Austen: Twentiety Century Views,* pp. 23-24.

2. Edmund Wilson, "A Long Talk about Jane Austen," in Watt, ed., *Jane Austen: Twentiety Century Views,* p. 37.

3. See Avrom Fleishman, *A Reading of Mansfield Park* (Baltimore: Johns Hopkins Press, 1967). I am indebted to this excellent study for an awareness of the religious overtones of the novel; the difference in our interpretations is that I view them as broadly ironic when placed in the social context.

4. Mary Lascelles, "Some Characteristics of Jane Austen's Style," *Essays and Studies,* 22 (1937):76-77.

5. *Mansfield Park* and *Bleak House* have much in common. Each uses for the first time in its author's career a neurotic character as exemplar: the Adlerian "feminine" personality type who develops submissive traits and hostile moral attitudes as self-protection. And each uses a house as the central metaphor of self-protection.

6. John Stuart Mill, *The Spirit of the Age,* ed. F. A. von Hayek (Chicago: University of Chicago Press, 1942), p. 6.

7. See Matthew Arnold's "Stanzas from the Grande Chartreuse" (1855), lines 85-88.

8. Thomas Carlyle, "Characteristics," in *Critical and Miscellaneous Essays,* ed. H. D. Traill (New York, 1896-1901), vol. 3.

9. For a detailed discussion of the historical suggestiveness of *Mansfield Park,* see Fleishman, *A Reading of Mansfield Park,* chap. 3.

10. Ibid.

11. Walter Houghton, *The Victorian Frame of Mind* (New Haven and London: Yale University Press, 1957), p. 343.

12. Yates is finally made "tolerably domestic and quiet."

13. Fleishman, *A Reading of Mansfield Park,* p. 67.

14. Ibid., p. 39. The abolition of slave trade in 1807 forbade slave shipments, not slavery, and was heavily felt in the British West Indies because the slaves did not survive and reproduce in sufficient numbers to provide a stable labor force; so it is very likely that Sir Thomas went to Antigua to improve the conditions of his slave population.

15. Lionel Trilling, *The Opposing Self* (New York: Viking, 1959), pp. 219-220.

16. For the background of this view of London see Frank Bradbrook, *Jane Austen and Her Predecessors* (Cambridge: Cambridge University Press, 1966), p. 39. The Gardiners of *Pride and Prejudice* are the cardinal exception; their London is not a hell.

17. Trilling, *The Liberal Imagination,* p. 208.

18. Sheila Kaye-Smith and G. B. Stern, *Speaking of Jane Austen* (New York and London: Harper and Brothers, 1944), p. 89.

19. The quasi-religious ethos of Mansfield calls to mind G. M. Young's suggestion that in the Victorian age "respectability" became the secular version of the evangelical religion.

20. Austen treats this implication with some irony, for in Fanny and Sir Thomas she examines the newly emerging strictness in the definitions of femininity and masculinity. Fanny represents the Victorian ideal of femininity, and she walks a thin line between passivity and resentment, piety and sanctimoniousness, obedience and subservience, chastity and prudishness, sensitivity and self-pity. Sir Thomas is the Victorian archetype of manhood as father, yet he too deviates between rationalism and worldliness, formality and coldness, sobriety and dullness. His long-winded, measured speech is satirized several times.

5. Civilization and the Contentment of *Emma*

1. E. M. Forster, *Abinger Harvest* (New York: Harcourt, Brace, and World, 1936), p. 148.

2. E. M. Forster, *Aspects of the Novel,* p. 66.

3. Hough, "Narrative and Dialogue in Jane Austen's *Emma,*" p. 220.

4. Ibid., pp. 219-220.

5. Mary Ellmann, *Thinking about Women* (New York: Harcourt, Brace, Jovanovich, 1968), p. 116.

6. Arnold Kettle, *An Introduction to the English Novel* (New York: Harper and Row, 1951), pp. 93-94.

7. Lionel Trilling, *Beyond Culture,* p. 57.

6. The Radical Pessimism of *Persuasion*

1. Lukács's description of novels that are halfway between "education" and "disillusionment."

2. That *Persuasion* is concerned with the nature of death as it is experienced by the living is revealed not only in passages concerning the dead or injured (Dick Musgrove, Fanny Harville, the young Musgrove whose collarbone is broken, Louisa Musgrove) but in the sheer quantity of widows and widowers in the novel: Sir Walter Elliot, Lady Russell, Mrs. Clay, Mr. Shepherd (we assume), Captain Benwick, Mr. Elliot, Mrs. Smith, Lady Dalrymple. Add to these those who are figuratively widowed: Anne, Elizabeth, and Captain Wentworth. How people bear up

under loss is therefore a consistent concern in *Persuasion* — and the loss can be of any kind; the novel opens with portraits of Sir Walter and Elizabeth trying to cope with their financial loss.

The sense of a human winter is persistent in *Persuasion*. The novel has an "end of life" feeling; it was written, of course, at the end of the author's life. There is in general a preoccupation with aging. Sir Walter continually comments on physical appearance; Lady Russell keeps her shades drawn when he visits to hide the crow's-feet around her eyes. In the fifteen or so years' absence from Anne, Mrs. Smith seems to have aged from girlhood to middle-aged convalescence. Anne's sense of aging is particularly keen, especially after Wentworth's mortifying comment that she was "so altered he should not have known her again." Anne possesses "every beauty excepting bloom" — a curious description in its association of beauty and death.

In *Persuasion,* the connection between evasion and persuasion is consistently examined. Everyone in the novel persuades himself in the face of misfortune, and the question arises (the question of a moralist, as Gilbert Ryle correctly insists): "When is persuasion evasion and when is it fortitude?" Sir Walter persuades himself for several years that he is financially secure; this is evasion, as is the Musgroves' grief over the son they did not care about when he was alive. Mrs. Smith's self-persuading cheerfulness is a form of fortitude, as Anne readily sees.

3. Marvin Mudrick, *Jane Austen: Irony as Defense and Discovery* (Berkeley and Los Angeles: University of California Press, 1968), p. 226.

4. At moments, this modern kind of ambiguity is finely achieved in *Persuasion,* such as the moment when Anne thinks Lady Russell has seen Wentworth from her carriage window at Bath. Lady Russell says instead that she has been looking at some curtains, and it is left up to the reader to decide whether Anne has fantasized it (*Per,* p. 179).

5. Lionel Trilling, *E.M. Forster* (Norfolk, Conn.: New Directions Books, 1943), p. 118.

6. Austen's language often turns on this paradox: "She was deep in the happiness of such misery, or the misery of such happiness" (*Per,* p. 229).

7. Quoted in Eiseley, *Darwin's Century,* p. 48.

7. Jane Austen as a Woman Writer

1. Even critics like Mark Schorer and Dorothy Van Ghent, who find Jane Austen's novels completely admirable, have thought it necessary to begin their essays with statements about the author's deliberate

limitation of her subject. For an interesting discussion of this tendency, see the section entitled "True but Trivial?" in E. Rubenstein's Introduction to *Twentieth Century Interpretations of Pride and Prejudice.*

2. Hough, "Narrative and Dialogue in Jane Austen's *Emma*," p. 228.

3. Ibid.

4. Ibid.

5. Southam, *Jane Austen,* p. 8.

6. Erik Erikson, "Inner and Outer Space: Reflections on Womanhood," *Daedalus,* 93, no. 2 (Spring 1964): 603.

7. G. M. Trevelyan, *A Shortened History of England* (Baltimore: Penguin, 1942), p. 385.

8. Wilson, "A Long Talk about Jane Austen."

9. Mudrick, *Jane Austen: Irony as Defense and Discovery,* p. 192.

10. Kettle, *An Introduction to the English Novel,* p. 98.

11. D. W. Harding, Introduction to *Persuasion,* Penguin English Library ed. (Baltimore, 1965), p. 14.

12. Matthew Arnold, "Selections form Matthew Arnold's Letters," in *Victorian Poetry and Poetics,* ed. Walter E. Houghton and G. Robert Stange (Boston: Houghton Mifflin, 1959), p. 551.

13. Mary Beard, *Woman as Force in History* (New York: Macmillan 1946), p. 308.

14. John Henry Raleigh, "What Scott Meant to the Victorians," *Victorian Studies* 7 (September 1963): 7-34.

15. Houghton, *The Victorian Frame of Mind,* pp. 341-394.

16. Ellmann, *Thinking about Women,* p. 116.

Index